MESSENGERS OF
HOPE

Also by David Bryant

In the Gap: What It Means to Be a World Christian

*The Hope at Hand: National and World Revival
for the Twenty-First Century*

*Concerts of Prayer: How Christians Can Join for Spiritual
Awakening and World Evangelization*

Stand in the Gap: How to Prepare for the Coming World Revival

MESSENGERS OF
H O P E

*BECOMING AGENTS OF REVIVAL
FOR THE TWENTY-FIRST CENTURY*

DAVID BRYANT

FOREWORD BY DR. JOHN M. PERKINS

Baker Books
A Division of Baker Book House Co
Grand Rapids, Michigan 49516

Published by Baker Books
a division of Baker Book House Company
P.O. Box 6287, Grand Rapids, MI 49516-6287

Printed in the United States of America

Library of Congress Cataloging-in-Publication Data
Bryant, David, 1945–
    Messengers of hope : becoming agents of revival for the twenty-first century / David Bryant.
        p. cm.
    Includes bibliographical references (p.).
    ISBN 0-8010-5785-X (pbk.)
    1. Church renewal. 2. Revivals. 3. Christianity—20th century. 4. Christianity—Forecasting. 5. Hope—Religious aspects—Christianity. 6. Bryant, David, 1945– . I. Title.
BV600.2.B78 1997
269′.24—dc21   97-22263

For current information about all releases from Baker Book House, visit our web site:
http://www.bakerbooks.com

To John and Lois Kyle

As a spiritual covering on my life, you have been God's message
from Christ to me, filling the years with unstoppable hope

CONTENTS

FOREWORD

B ack in the late 1960s, one of the few white churches to get behind our emerging Voice of Calvary ministry in Jackson, Mississippi, was pastored by a twentysomething young man named David Bryant. Now, nearly thirty years later, I have the privilege of commending to you wholeheartedly his latest book, *Messengers of Hope*.

Let me say right up front, I share with David an increasing hope that a genuine biblical revival is about to unfold in our nation. As we've discussed at National Prayer Committee meetings (which David chairs and on which I serve), the Spirit of God is obviously at work to that end. Already early stages of this revival can be seen in national stirrings among Christian teens, in renewal initiatives like the great Promise Keepers men's events, in new expressions of commitment toward racial reconciliation and healing in the church, in the creative urban ministries for Christ taking shape in our major cities, and in widespread movements of united prayer for revival and spiritual awakening.

David Bryant has been in the thick of these developments for nearly twenty years. Truly, he is what this book is titled: a Messenger of Hope. More specifically, through his Concerts of Prayer International, David and his team have made a significant difference. The most exciting urban ministries I see today are based on and nourished by Concerts of Prayer gatherings and united prayer events. For example, David and his staff have focused for years on New York City, helping the prayer movement there become a model for others who want to seek God for the four great spiritual needs of our cities: revival in the church, reconciliation among the races, reformation of society, and reaching the lost.

But as David writes, one such "messenger" is not enough. I agree with him: "The time has come to flood our nation with Messengers of Hope." Many, both clergy and laypeople—reconciled across race and denomination—must help spread the news of God's great promises to us in Christ for spiritual awakening in our land. To be sure, the Holy Spirit is the primary Agent of Revival. But in every one of America's great awakenings in the past three hundred years, he has been pleased to use men and women who gave themselves to join the Holy Spirit as his agents of revival.

In fact, one of the unique contributions of *Messengers of Hope* is David's acknowledged indebtedness (as a White author) to the historic African-American church as a rich depository of God-centered hope and a message of hope. As you'll discover, he begins each chapter by quoting extensively from Black Christian leaders over the past two hundred years, who again and again reassure us that biblical hope empowers, enriches, and transforms any generation. There's no doubt that many African-American believers today are poised to be agents of revival for the whole body of Christ. What an incentive to keep working at racial reconciliation.

Following on the heels of its companion volume *(The Hope at Hand: National and World Revival for the Twenty-First Century)*, *Messengers of Hope* lifts up the vision for revival, lays out the biblical rationale for being messengers of this hope, and inspires all of us to take strong initiatives, under Christ, to be God's agents of revival. But David gives us more. The second half of his book spells out, in the most practical ways, how every Christian can fulfill his or her calling to be such an agent in a variety of settings. There's something here for everyone.

It is my hope and prayer that I will yet see, with my own eyes, the full spiritual awakening for which many of us have labored for decades. I firmly believe I will! But it will not come without hope-filled messengers. Daily I seek to be one of them. And *you* can be one of them too. David Bryant will show you how.

Dr. John M. Perkins
President, Foundation for Reconciliation and Development

ACKNOWLEDGMENTS

In a sense this volume was already written two years ago. It was in my heart even as I penned *The Hope at Hand.* To be honest, I was tempted to shoehorn it into that book. But better sense prevailed. The topic deserved a thorough treatment by itself. Now, here it is. I want to thank Baker Book House, and especially senior editor Dan Van't Kerkhoff, for their enthusiastic backing of my effort to turn one book into two. What a terrific publisher Baker is in every way!

I'm also indebted to many "messengers of hope" who have enriched my life during the past three years of my teaching on this topic. Because of them I now have so much more to say. I've met thousands of them in major prayer events (like fasting and prayer convocations and youth concerts of prayer), in Promise Keepers rallies, at clergy training conferences, and through the multitude of daily contacts at Concerts of Prayer International.

My deep appreciation to the board of directors, my ministry team (scattered between Chicago and New York), our National Board of Advocates, and countless intercessors and supporters—all dedicated to the vision of Concerts of Prayer International. With me they share the mission of fostering united prayer movements worldwide and flooding the body of Christ with messengers of the hope of revival.

Special gratitude goes to my family—to my three dear ones (Adam, Bethany, Benjamin) who give me reason to hope every day, and to my precious wife, Robyne, who not only did all the entry and helpful editing on this book, but who has learned with me to "abound in hope by the power of the Holy Spirit" (Rom. 15:13 NRSV) for nearly thirty years.

All of these people join with me in offering this book up to our Lord, Jesus Christ, the one who *is* the Messenger of Hope, *the* promise-filled agent of revival for the twenty-first century.

Helps from Concerts of Prayer International

The Hope at Hand

NATIONAL AND WORLD REVIVAL FOR THE TWENTY-FIRST CENTURY

Our troubled nation is beset by violent crime, broken families, and deteriorating cities. Nevertheless, praying Christians everywhere are beginning to share a new hope for our generation.

This rising hope is for nothing less than national and world revival. When—not if—it comes, says author David Bryant, the church will awaken dramatically in repentance, righteousness, and service. Obstacles to the gospel will crumble so quickly we won't be able to keep up with the story of what God is doing. And the resulting wave of global evangelization will reach millions of people who have never been reached before.

In this inspiring volume, you'll read about thrilling new indications that the beginning of this revival is upon us. You'll learn of a growing grassroots prayer movement springing up among pastors and laypeople all across America. And most of all, you'll discover how you can play a part in anticipating, encouraging, and experiencing this coming revival in your own life and the life of your congregation.

David Bryant is founder and president of Concerts of Prayer International, an organization that works with numbers of national and international evangelical networks committed to prayer mobilization, revival, and world evangelization. He has also spent years studying the characteristics of historic revival. His wide travels and broad connections across denominational and multi-ethnic lines, and his role as chairman of America's National Prayer Committee, put him in a unique position to recognize and herald the signs of a coming spiritual awakening for our day. As he explains, God is not only willing and able to send awakening—he is ready.

This book is must reading for any believer who wants to understand what is about to happen and play a vital role in bringing it about more quickly.

Take It to Your Friends

SMALL GROUP STUDY/DISCUSSION GUIDE TO THE HOPE AT HAND

This excellent twelve-part, sixty-four-page study guide makes it easy to share the hope for spiritual awakening with others. Written by David Bryant as a companion piece to his book *The Hope at Hand*, it provides you with an easy way to study this material on your own or with others.

Each one-hour session is carefully designed to help incite new hope for global awakening to Christ and to involve group members in a response that will deepen their personal hope for what is ahead. Thought-provoking discussion questions, life application steps, and how-to's on revival praying make this an excellent basis for powerful study for your small group or Sunday school class.

Write, call, or fax:

Concerts of Prayer International
P.O. Box 1399
Wheaton, IL 60189
Phone: 630-690-8441
Fax: 630-690-0160
24-hour toll free request line: 1-800-576-6458

THE OPERATIVE WORD IS *HOPE*

Few in our generation have yet experienced one of God's greatest gifts to his church—*revival*. Nevertheless, we know with certainty what one major characteristic of a coming spiritual awakening will be. Past Spirit-shaped revivals have manifested themselves in many unique ways across centuries, cultures, and traditions. Yet one common theme has marked them all: They are periods of immense hope.

The cause for that hope is undisputed. Times of revival are hope-filled because they are spiritual awakenings to Christ. Discussion of spiritual subjects or an increase in faith-related activities is all well and good. But an interest or appreciation for the spiritual alone has no power to change. Only Christ himself can truly transform individual lives, churches, cities, and nations. At the very core of hope is the anticipation of a brighter future. Only Christ has the power to bring genuine, lasting transformation to his people and the world. That is why any true spiritual revival—one that is hope-filled—must be an awakening to Jesus Christ. It is time to experience that kind of hope again. Worldwide, Christian leaders believe we are entering a day of such revival. I concur. Revival is at hand.[1] This book is dedicated to helping you play a key role in ushering in what will be the most exciting days you will ever know.

Historically, a critical catalyst in all awakenings has been Christians acting as "agents of revival." The centuries brim with millions of them. Their primary role has usually been twofold: (1) to be messengers of the hope of revival, and (2) to be mobilizers of concerted prayer for revival. I have already written extensively on the topic of united prayer for revival.[2] I now turn enthusiastically to the exploration of why and how we must become Messengers of Hope. Please join me!

Do Not Be Afraid

In his book *Crossing the Threshold of Hope,* Pope John Paul II summarizes his relentless confidence in what God is doing in our generation. This hope for the future is based in part on firsthand observations he has made since 1978 on sixty-two missionary trips around the globe.[3] His thesis is simple: If we understand biblical Christianity correctly, it can only lead us into greater hope.

Just a few miles from my home, the pope repeated to an audience of one hundred thousand in Giants Stadium a phrase that dominates his book: "Do not be afraid!" A few hours later, appearing before the United Nations General Assembly, he challenged world leaders to conquer their fears and to rediscover in God a spirit of immense hope to carry us into the twenty-first century.

His message recalls for me the opening words of Dietrich Bonhoeffer's *Creation and Fall:* "The Church of Christ bears witness to the end of all things. It lives from the end, it thinks from the end, it acts from the end, it proclaims its message from the end. . . . Christ is the new, Christ is the end of the old. . . . Therefore, the Scriptures need to be read and proclaimed wholly from the viewpoint of the end."[4]

Both of these men are convinced that because of Christ, Christians have a liberating message of hope for our generation, one of global and eternal magnitude. If any segment of the church, however, has a greater right and responsibility to declare to the world, "Do not be afraid," surely it is the evangelical movement. "The most dynamic energized sector of religion has been the evangelical one, and its eschatological vision is central."[5] In other words, committed Christians always thrive under the compulsion of the consummation. It is not an issue of being "otherworldly" but rather "future-worldly."[6] God has told us how the future will conclude. That knowledge cannot help but impact the way we choose to move along the path to that future.

Despite the fact that many today are caught up with "apocalyptic fever," anticipating our entrance into the third millennium, we must never disparage the legitimate revolutionary impact a message of hope can have on any of us. In fact, we might argue that a vision for the future (eschatology) "is the most pastoral of all theological perspectives, showing how the ending impinges on the present,"[7] helping us boldly seize the present, flush with the dawning of God's new day—the consummation—just ahead of us. The sunrise of Christ's resurrection and ascension, the outpouring of the Holy Spirit at Pentecost, and the certain knowledge of Christ's return and rule intersect our every move. Our calling in Christ and the importance of our message to the world make every risk and sacrifice as God's messengers worthwhile.

Each fulfillment of God's promises to the church and among the nations incites us to even greater hope for the future. The Christian life rises from faith to faith, from promise to promise, from glory to glory—from hope to hope (Rom. 4:13–25).

Hope Is a Virtue

Noted intellectual Richard John Neuhaus has said, "The times may be bad, but they are the only times we are given. Remember, hope is still a Christian virtue, and despair is a mortal sin."[8] The power of this hope has been demonstrated dramatically by Spirit-led Christians throughout the ages.

In the fourteenth century, Dr. John Wycliffe, a brilliant Oxford scholar, burned with a passion to spread the hope of Christ throughout England by translating the Scriptures into the common vernacular. At the center of controversy throughout much of his life and condemned by the church as a heretic, Wycliffe refused to heed his enemies' sanctions on his preaching. From his deathbed in exile, he commissioned scores of itinerant priests to proclaim Christ throughout Europe. Historians call him the "morning star" of one of history's greatest revivals, the Reformation. A near-contemporary chronicler of Wycliffe's life observed:

> They burned his bones to ashes and cast them into the Swift, a neighboring brook running hard by. Thus, this brook hath conveyed his ashes to Avon, Avon into Seven, Seven into the Nallow Seas, they into the main ocean. And thus the ashes of Wycliffe are the emblem of his doctrine, which now is disbursed the world over.[9]

In our own generation, Pastor Christian Fuhrer is another who stands as a shining example of what hope-filled determination in God's supreme authority can do. Fuhrer lived in the former East Germany under an oppressive and godless regime. All around him he saw signs of hopelessness and despair. Daily provisions could only be obtained by standing in long lines. The rate of alcoholism among adults was dangerously high. His profession placed him under scrutiny by a cold and iron-fisted government. Yet he was hopeful! Certainly, this hope was not based on circumstances. Nor could it have come from his own personal, spiritual resources. Fuhrer's confidence in the future came from God himself. And not only did he have hope, he became a messenger of hope.

Throughout the 1980s, each evening at 5:00 P.M., Pastor Fuhrer led East German believers in prayers for peace. In defiance of all human reason, believers in East Berlin became so infected with hope they literally filled the streets with hymns and prayers. Ultimately, without a revolution, without a shot being fired, the fall of the Berlin Wall became a physical representation of the dismantling of the communist government.

What a modern-day messenger of hope! Fuhrer reminds us, "As Christians we are called always to hope. We should expect the unexpected and not let despair get the best of us."[10]

What insights do these men and other messengers of hope through the ages have to share with us today? They understand our relationship to Christ is not only a positional one, it is also a *directional* one. As Christians we don't stand frozen in place, communicating with God at a standstill. We *follow* Christ. And where is he going? Into the future. Our circumstances and surroundings simply cannot shape our expectations for tomorrow. Where God is involved, we must recognize and communicate hope for tomorrow.

British pastor Martyn Lloyd-Jones concurred. As he wrote in his book on revival, "The great and constant danger is that we should be content with something which is altogether less than that intended for us."[11] Throughout his ministry in the mid 1900s, he consistently wrote and preached a central truth: "When we are dealing with God, we must always be prepared for the unexpected."[12] Another messenger of hope.

In the summer of 1996, such a spirit of expectation vividly unfolded before my eyes in the city of Seoul, Korea. I was speaking at the Global Conference on World Evangelization (GCOWE), an event that summoned nearly four thousand leaders of world missions from over two hundred nations. Two meetings during that conference stand out in my mind. First, nearly seventy thousand university students converged in Olympic Stadium to spend six hours (in a driving rainstorm!) looking at the challenge of world evangelization, embracing the hope that it could be done, and committing themselves to believe that God would do it through people like them. At the conclusion, after a forty-five-minute concert of prayer, over sixty thousand offered themselves *in writing* to go anywhere God would send them to complete the task. That is how filled with confidence they were about God's future for the nations!

Amazingly, an even more dramatic moment occurred the following evening. All four thousand GCOWE delegates reconvened to spend an evening in worship and prayer. What took place may be unique in the history of the church. Mission strategists, representing most nations and most major denominations, lifted up their voices as one to cry out to God for a worldwide outpouring of the Holy Spirit to bring forth a revival for the twenty-first century. We prayed these prayers in the hope and realization that only such an awakening would secure the fulfillment of the Great Commission. Why did we pray like that? Because after days of cooperative planning, we were filled with assurance that Christ would be victorious in his mission, and that we were to be a part of that victory with him—right now!

It is manifestations of hope such as these that have caused many to conclude that evangelicalism is really the future of Protestantism in the world. The reason is simple: "Head and heart are being brought together in a movement that is looking forward to the future with a sense of expectancy and anticipation."[13] As evangelical Christians, *hope* is our operative word.

In 1995, when Christian statesman Leighton Ford was asked to give a charge to a new generation of leaders for the next century, he wrote that his prayer was for them to become "hopers." He said, "God is always ahead of us and moving us on. And so as you minister in a world often steeped in confusion and despair, I hope you will breathe expectancy. God always has another move!"[14]

To breathe the air of expectancy and to communicate God's Word and his works with a holy anticipation of so much more—that is what it means to be a Messenger of Hope.

Biblical Hope Is an Abounding Hope

The one overarching demand the gospel makes of *all* of us is this: Put your hope in God. "In this simple act of hope his grace is glorified, and sinners are saved. This is the command of the gospel that keeps God at the center—the center of his affections and ours."[15] He is not only the God who is and was, but also the God "who is to come" (Rev. 1:8). Over seventy-five hundred promises crisscross the Bible. And all of them say "Yes!" to those of us in Christ—guaranteed (2 Cor. 1:20).

My own years of study convince me that Scripture's promises can be summarized into *six* dynamic dimensions of the work of Christ: who he is to us, for us, over us, within us, through us, and most relevant to this book, who he is out ahead of us. Out ahead of us? Yes. True, some promises have already been fulfilled. Most, however, have not yet been realized—not fully, because they await the consummation. But in a preliminary sense, all of God's promises can be proclaimed to be "at hand," bearing down on top of us, ready to break through in marvelous approximations of how they will ultimately be fulfilled in the consummation. Fresh installments of the new creation await all of our churches and missions. Today, Christ goes before us to take us there. As I said before, we *follow* him. That's why *hope* is the operative word.

Ephesians 1:18 and 4:4 assure us that all Christians are defined by the same hope. We've been born again to a living hope through the resurrection of Jesus Christ (1 Peter 1:3). Fixing our hope on the promise of even more grace coming at us (1 Peter 1:13), we are ready to answer any who ask us where our life of confident expectation comes from (1 Peter 3:15–16). Anticipating greater manifestations of God's glory, we constantly rejoice (Rom. 5:3). Our hearts are so possessed with God's love for us that we renounce fears that he will somehow fail to fulfill all that he has promised (Rom. 5:5). Our God longs to do exceedingly above and beyond what we could ask or think (Eph. 3:20–21), and to surprise us with awesome deeds of righteousness. How can we not pronounce him to be the hope for all the ends of the earth (Ps. 65:5)?

Repeatedly, God reassures us of his plans for us—plans to prosper us and to give us a hope and a future (Jer. 29:10–11). This is the motivation for seeking him with all our hearts (Jer. 29:13).

Take a look at the Sermon on the Mount. As with many commands of Scripture, it is infused with promised rewards. The Beatitudes, for example, make little sense apart from the hope of God's sovereign, gracious intervention for those who seek him (described in the second half of each Beatitude). Once that hope is present, saints are eager to take whatever steps are needed to fulfill God's plan. As Henri Nouwen puts it, "Hope prevents us from clinging to what we have and frees us to move away from the safe place and enter unknown and fearful territory."[16]

When a whole congregation of people for whom all this is true come together, the hallmark of a truly Spirit-filled church is demonstrated—an *abounding* hope, produced by the power of the Holy Spirit (Rom. 15:13). Prepare for it!

What Hope Is Not

Now, let's be clear on three points. First, biblical hope does not walk with *presumption.* An excess of confidence in one's self and what one can accomplish eventually leads to downfall and disaster. Nor should we presume that all our own dreams or ambitions—even for Christ—are necessarily given or guaranteed by God. We should also realize we cannot assume that the fulfillment of God's promises is inevitable in the face of persistent sin or unbelief. If we grieve the Holy Spirit, we have no right to expect to abound in his power.

Second, biblical hope is the opposite of *resignation*. It is more like a rebellion against the status quo—a summons into a Christ-centered revolution. To hope in God is not to escape from reality; rather it is to have the courage to look reality straight in the eye. The moment we hold is not final in Christ. God has much more for us; we won't settle for less.

This is a major message of the apocalyptic parts of the Bible, including Daniel, Ezekiel, and Revelation. Filled with radical (though sometimes enigmatic) visions of the future, these passages dramatize a hope taught in much of Scripture: No matter how dark the circumstances may seem, righteousness triumphs. The kingdom comes at God's decree, not man's. Even at our darkest moments, God's redemptive judgments are accelerating toward the fulfillment of all his promises. In turn, God's people are to prepare for this coming hope, to live lives consistent with it right now, to be marked by a spirit of watchfulness and waiting, coupled with urgency, to be a people of hope until God intervenes to do for them what they are not able to do for themselves.

Finally, *optimism* is not a synonym for biblical hope. (Someone defined an optimist as a Yugo owner with a car alarm!) In his commentary on Revelation, Eugene Peterson observes that "human optimism comes in two forms: moral and technological. The moral optimist thinks that generous applications of well-intentioned goodwill to the slag heaps of injustice, wickedness, and the world's corruption will put the world gradually, but surely, in the right." I wonder how many Christians also engage life with this well-intentioned goodwill that falls so far short of the Spirit-induced hope that can ultimately set things right? Peterson goes on: "The technological optimist thinks that by vigorously applying scientific intelligence to the problems of poverty, pollution, and neurosis, the world will gradually, but surely, be put right." Any technological optimists serving on your local church's leadership council? Peterson concludes: "Neither form of optimism worships God. . . . Optimists see that there are a few things left to do to get the world in good shape and think they are just the ones to do it."[17]

Why is it so essential to avoid presumption, resignation, and optimism? Why strive to lay hold of the dynamic dimensions of biblical hope? Well, remember the people around Jesus who ultimately crucified him; they were people of distorted vision. The results were not pretty. The Pharisees anchored their future to the success of their own "lay renewal movement," pushing the nation back to full commitment to Moses and the law. The Sadducees took their name from the high priestly family of Zadok, Ezekiel's envisioned leadership for the promised new temple. Unfortunately, the Sadducees tied their self-assumed destiny to an uneasy compromise with the secular powers of Rome. Judas probably betrayed Jesus out of his own impatience with how ineffectively Jesus seemed to be fulfilling the hope he proclaimed. Desperate for more immediate results, Judas offered Jesus to the Sanhedrin in the hopes of forcing Jesus' hand. Preserving his prospects in the face of the inflamed masses was Pilate's goal. How? Eliminate all competition to his future ambitions. And the crowd? They cheered Jesus in his triumphal entry, raising the great prayer for revival, "Hosanna!" which means literally, "Lord, save us now!" But how quickly they retrograded into the security of tradition and ancient rituals, too preoccupied to sustain their involvement through the end of the week. Clearly, Neuhaus is right: Lack of hope, true biblical hope, can be a mortal sin.

Jesus, however, broke through all these deceptions and lies, the greatest of all being idolatrous pride. Taking the mortal sin of misplaced hopes into his own body on the cross, he rose again to subsume in himself every promise God had ever offered to those who hope in him. He is the consummation itself, our blessed hope (Titus 2:13) and our glory: "the glorious riches of this mystery, which is Christ in you, the hope of glory" (Col. 1:27). He is also our message of hope, the focus of the coming revival.

Signs of Hope in Hong Kong

Beautiful Hong Kong Stadium looks out over a world-class city. In 1995, I watched ten thousand Hong Kong believers gather there for a three-hour concert of prayer to intercede for their homeland, which was about to revert to the control of mainland Chinese communists. That afternoon I preached on the hope-filled promise of Jeremiah 33:3: "Call to me and I will answer you and tell you great and unsearchable things you do not know." I told them that God is always ready to unleash a fresh work in our lives (or in our city), one that goes way beyond what we have seen him do before. In fact, Jeremiah 33 was spoken to a helpless prophet sitting in prison inside a city under siege, yet, amazingly, the whole chapter is about the hope of revival! God showed Jeremiah a transformed community, awash with spiritual awakening, experiencing grace upon grace.

That afternoon, huddled under umbrellas in a Pacific rainstorm, Hong Kong believers cried out to God with renewed assurance that he would give them in principle a Jeremiah 33–style revival in the coming years. Their praying crackled with anticipation of God's renewal for Hong Kong. They saw a church galvanized to be a base of operations for Christ's kingdom throughout the Chinese world. They chose to pray (and obey) with a hope requiring them "to believe in advance what will only make sense in reverse."[18]

Such is the heartbeat of this book. But the signs are also close to home.

An African-American Legacy

I've been at work many years proclaiming the hope of revival. Eager Christians along the way have deepened and sharpened that message within me. A multitude of heralds, including a host of prayer mobilizers all throughout the body of Christ, have nourished within me unstoppable expectations toward God.

But the segment of the church that has had the most profound impact on my vision has been the African-American church. Theirs is a body supremely marked by hope. As African-American scholar Stephen Carter writes, "Black Americans are the most religious, the most devout people in the world."[19] This devotion overflows in abounding hope. It is the kind of hope discovered by Jonathan Kozol in the South Bronx, where hope-filled churches are the survivors, evidencing an "amazing grace" that sustains people in the face of overwhelming poverty.[20]

It's the kind of hope expressed by Bishop George McKinney, leader of a major inner-city church in San Diego, who reflects: "With God bringing all peoples to our city, this could be the Black Church's finest hour to catch the vision to reach across racial and ethnic lines. The Black Church is best equipped with how to deal with the urban crisis, because we have been in the crucible of pain."[21] Speaking out of his own context, Tony Evans captures Black hope quite simply: "The church must penetrate the culture with the message, 'You're going down, but look up. In your distress cry to the Lord. Seek him, and he will let you find him.'"[22] In his effort to groom God-centered leaders in the Black community, theologian Samuel D. Proctor writes in his book *The Substance of Things Hoped For: A Memoir of African-American Faith* that the African-American experience has created a faith that "puts steel in our spines to endure physical bondage, and zeal in our souls to prevail against evil; it illuminates our minds to hold on to a vision of a better day and inspires our hearts to learn."[23]

My indebtedness to these brothers and sisters in Christ was inescapable to me as we concluded a recent Messenger of Hope Conference held in a Black inner-city church in Seattle. For two days, spiritual leaders from throughout the Pacific Northwest met together. The two hundred participants, many of them pastors, represented a healthy mixture of Black and White Christians. We set aside the final session for dedicating ourselves to be messengers of hope. But God indicated he wanted us to alter the approach. All the White pastors came forward to kneel at the front of the sanctuary. All the Black pastors were invited to stand before them, to lay on hands, and to pray prayers of recommission. Why? Because our two days of discussions had convinced us that the message of revival we needed to proclaim into all our churches was already alive and pulsing in many of the African-American churches represented among us. Our prayer was that the Spirit of abounding hope (Rom. 15:13), already resting vitally on Black congregations and leaders, might come upon all of us (as Moses and his elders experienced in Num. 11:25), so each one could return to his or her own people to be an effective agent of revival. It was a profound moment for me.

As you'll see, I've begun a number of chapters with prayers drawn from the book *Conversations with God: Two Centuries of Prayers by African-Americans.*[24] This is so you, too, might catch something of the message of hope that has so powerfully dominated the Black Christian experience for generations. What a legacy they give to the coming revival!

Here's Where We're Headed

Messengers of Hope begins where I left off in *The Hope at Hand.* In that companion volume, I discussed reasons why we can pray and prepare with absolute confidence that a God-given revival of national and global proportions is coming to the church for the twenty-first century. Since publishing it, the signs of revival have increased markedly.

This can be seen in the movement of prayer for revival throughout the body of Christ. As I've often said, there are many feeder streams of prayer into the riverbed of coming revival. The full river of revival may not be here yet, but the feeder streams (local, national, and international prayer initiatives) are very active. Thus, it is only right to conclude—since we serve a prayer-initiating, prayer-answering God—that the *river* of revival cannot be far behind! Which alerts us to the critical need of the hour. God's praying people (and there are millions of them) must be kept as clear as possible on the hope we are praying toward.

That need shapes the central thesis for this book. Now that the prayer movement is up and rolling, we must flood our nation (beginning with the body of Christ) with messengers of hope. These are the agents who will keep the true hope of revival—awakening to Jesus Christ—clear and central for the prayer movement until our prayers are fully answered. These are the ones who will help us better prepare to run with the answers to our prayers as they come. In fact, these messengers themselves are a major answer to all our prayers.

In Psalm 68:11, we read: "The Lord announced the word, and great was the company of those who proclaimed it." Have you heard Handel's *Messiah* recently? Do you remember the chorus based on this verse? Handel captures musically the drama of what is pictured in Psalm 68. First, he has all the men sing quite forcefully in unison: "The Lord gave the word." Then, the entire choir takes up the second half of the verse, "and great was the company of the preachers." Each section of the choir sings this same refrain in different directions, giving us the feel of a multitude of messengers scattering across the landscape, carrying everywhere the hope first announced by God.

And what is that word? It is nothing less than the promise of revival. Seen in the context of Psalm 68, which begins in verse 1 with the phrase "May God arise, may his enemies be scattered," the word is that enemy kings and armies have fled in haste; that God's triumphal procession is moving through the enemy camp, taking booty and captives; that the triumphant parade is ascending Zion's hill into the temple—all so that God may manifest his glorious presence before his people as they celebrate the victory with him. It's all about revival, biblical revival, pure and simple. As verse 11 tells us, when the Lord gives the word that a revival is at hand, messengers of hope carry the good news throughout the church. Actually, they aren't able to stop themselves!

Today, once again, God is raising up an army of heralds. In part, this book is a result of my meetings with thousands of them while teaching on this subject. I have encountered present and potential messengers of hope in scores of pastors' seminars and regional conferences, as well as in training times with young people and lay leaders throughout the churches.

True, many with whom I have met are clergy. But agents of revival can also be found among the laity of thousands of local congregations. Preeminent are the praying people, those who have sought the Lord for years for the river that's coming. But many others are joining now in the proclamation of hope even as you read these pages. It is these messengers of hope who will significantly determine how God's people prepare for and enter into a God-given revival for the twenty-first century.

Revival is our message of hope. Even more accurately, our message is Christ, who is at the center of revival. "Faith comes from hearing the message, and the message is heard through the word of Christ" (Rom. 10:17). Jesus guarantees the "much more" God wants to do in us, through us, and out ahead of us. As discussed in depth in *The Hope at Hand*, Christ-centered revival is the foremost manifestation of the hope God offers to any generation of his people. It's the greatest blessing we can anticipate apart from and until the second coming.

Throughout this book we will see why so many are convinced that God is not only willing and able, but ready *right now* to bring spiritual awakening to believers throughout the church. Actually, the initial purpose of this book is to make you a "prisoner" of such hope (see chapter 3), and to help you get free of what I call "boxes of pea-sized Christianity" (see my book *Stand in the Gap*).[25] I want you to live a confident discipleship that is hope-filled from beginning to end.

Most of all, I'm writing to equip you to be a messenger of this hope to others. Part of that equipping involves finding new confidence to proclaim such a message (see chapter 4). But part of it (the focus of the second half of this book) also requires practical skills that will help you effectively deliver this message to your family, your small group Bible study, your Sunday school class, or your congregation on a Sunday morning. We'll explore four critical ingredients that need to be a part of every message of hope (chapters 7 through 10), and will also talk about how Christ is the center of our message of hope, uncovering guidelines to help you keep him there (chapter 6).

The Blade of the Sickle

In 1986, while serving as minister-at-large for InterVarsity Christian Fellowship, I helped guide a celebration at Mount Hermon, Massachusetts, commemorating the hundredth anniversary of a student Bible conference led by Dwight L. Moody. That gathering in August of 1886 precipitated the unprecedented Student Volunteer Movement. Out of extended study on God's magnificent promises and seasons of prayer, one hundred students propelled a missionary recruitment effort that lasted for over thirty years and sent out some twenty thousand new missionaries overseas. It was also a catalyst for the Laymen's Missionary Movement, which by the early 1900s supplied funding for enlarging the North American missionary thrust. A century later, in

1986, 250 of us gathered to revisit this gracious movement and to honor the agents of revival it produced for a whole generation.

The day after our conference, after everyone had gone home, I wandered down the hillside from the conference grounds. Strolling along the Connecticut River, I pondered what God had done in 1886, and whether he was willing to do it again. Following the old path, I came upon a cornfield, full and ripe for the late August harvest. From where I stood, it seemed to stretch to the horizon. As I gazed, however, the stalks of corn with leaves raised up toward the sun suggested to me a great army of Christians, row upon row, offering praises to God. Then, in my mind's eye, all the stalks were suddenly cut off at the ground, falling forward as it were, in worshipful surrender to the Lord. In prayer, I asked God how this could happen. What was the sickle applied to reap this harvest of freshly dedicated Christians? The answer came immediately: the movement of prayer for revival, already rapidly unfolding across the nation. I responded with another question: If the sickle itself was the prayer movement, what was the sharpened blade of the sickle? Again, an answer came: The blade itself was a message of hope—the hope of revival. Finally, I wondered: Who will swing the sickle? But I had no need to ask. I knew the answer. The same as it had been one hundred years ago. Messengers of Hope!

In the years since that experience, by firsthand observation across the globe, I see that this is precisely what God is up to. He is reaping a whole new army of decisively devoted believers, moving out for the global cause of Christ. To accomplish this harvest, the revival movement requires the sickle of the prayer movement and the blade of the message of hope. As God's people pray, hearing that message and seeking God for mighty things that they have not yet seen, full spiritual awakening will come upon us. At the forefront of the awakened hosts will be the harvesters—the agents of revival, the messengers of hope.

This book is about the blade of the sickle. It's about those who swing the sickle. It's about how they do it. And in it all the operative word is *hope*.

Part One

The Messenger

The nation sleeps, Jehovah, Jove.
Thou Archive of incarnate love,
Our first, Beginning, Middle, End,
Thou man's Creator, Father, Friend.
Alpha, Omega, Source of Light,
Great God, Immortal, Infinite,
Exhaustless Fountain, Highest, Best,
Eternal Rock of Righteousness . . .

Our Life, our Hope, our Guide, our Reed,
Our Refuge in the time of need,
Thou Dazzling Sun, incline Thine ear
Unto Thy Servant's humble prayer.

Eternal God, Thy grace impart,
Look down in pity, Thou who art
The Ruler of the universe,
We pray Thee, Lord, remove the curse
Of hate and prejudice that stand
With ill design and fiery brand
Men's hearts to torture; on a race
Of helpless creatures, turn Thy face.

O God, this sleeping nation wake . . .

Maurice N. Corbett,
"Appeal to Heaven" (1914),
taken from *Conversations with God:
Two Centuries of Prayers by African-Americans*

CHAPTER ONE

A NATION IN NEED OF MESSENGERS OF HOPE

It was a warm May day in Washington, D.C., as I sat among seven hundred other specially invited guests in the rotunda of our nation's Capitol Building. Before congressional, diplomatic, and religious leaders, Dr. and Mrs. Billy Graham were about to be presented with the Congressional Gold Medal. Rising to receive this honor, Dr. Graham's words of acceptance were unexpected by many sitting before him. In contrast to the ceremony and self-congratulations that accompany so many occasions of man honoring man, his message cut swiftly through pomp. In a brief speech entitled "The Hope for America," he said:

> During this century we have witnessed the outer limits of human evil. Our mood on the brink of the twenty-first century is far more somber. . . . there is much about America that is no longer good. You know the problems as well as I do: racial and ethnic tensions that threaten to rip apart our cities and neighborhoods, crime and violence of epidemic proportions in most of our cities, children taking weapons to school, broken families, poverty, drugs, teenage pregnancy, corruption, the list is almost endless. . . . We have confused liberty with license—and we are paying the awful price. We are a society poised on the brink of self destruction. . . . What is the cure? Is there any hope? *Yes. There is hope!* Our lives can be changed and our world can be

changed. . . . if ever we needed God's help, it is now. If ever we needed spiritual renewal, it is now.[1]

In that one moment, two things were clearly illustrated. We are a nation in desperate need of hope. And the time has come to flood the land with many messengers of hope.

A World Bereft of Hope

Samuel Johnson noted, "Hope is the chief happiness which this world offers." What kind of hope does our world offer our generation right now? According to Bill Gates's inaugural book, *The Road Ahead*, we can anticipate a world dominated by extraordinary technological advances. He is convinced these will make all of us smarter, happier, faster, and better. Much of this hope for him, of course, is linked to the success of an "Information Super-highway."[2]

Evangelical statesman and theologian Carl F. H. Henry, however, sees it differently. He says we live in "a world bereft of hope."[3] Many are inclined to agree. From his years of travel in mass evangelism, Luis Palau notes that "a spirit of despondency lies over the nation. We've lost hope."[4] Chatting with former Secretary of Education William Bennett, Chuck Colson was asked: "Tell me, can you name one positive trend in our culture?" Colson was caught by surprise. After a few moments of silence he had to admit that he was not able to come up with even a single hopeful cultural indicator.[5]

This blanket of hopelessness may relate, in part, to America's frantic pace of life, directly responsible for increases in hypertension, heart disease, and psychological disabilities such as depression. Many of us are simply overwhelmed by the amount of information we're required to process and use daily. It is estimated that human knowledge is expanding at the rate of six hundred million words *each hour!*[6] Keeping up in even a small way leaves us little time to reflect on the present, let alone dream great expectations for the future. One-quarter of Americans say that they feel utterly exhausted, frazzled by the lack of time, and literally on the breaking point. Burnout![7] We are physically and emotionally depleted. What kind of hope can a person in that condition muster?

Other plagues on our society also continue to rob us of hope.

The crime rate has increased nearly 1,000 percent since 1950, with a 560 percent increase in violent crime since 1960.

One in five Americans is infected with an incurable sexually transmitted disease, the fruits of a borderless hedonism. (Be merry—tomorrow we die! What hope is that?)

Depletion of the ozone, the possibly disastrous greenhouse effect, and other environmental disruptions are now major concerns.

The diminishing of the value of human life is obvious in what many term "killing for convenience"—abortion, assisted suicides, euthanasia, fetal tissue research.

The erosion of trust and growing disillusionment toward political, religious, and other leadership in our land causes us to despair. How can we have hope when those leading us into the future have so often failed to earn our confidence?

The general erosion of our inner cities, with its resulting ravages on interpersonal relations causes millions of urban Americans to have a pervasive sense of loneliness and isolation.

One bastion of hopelessness is found among the thirty-six million Americans living in poverty. That number is equivalent to every man, woman, and child in the twenty-five largest cities—one out of every seven Americans. It includes twelve million kids who suffer from chronic daily hunger, over 330,000 of whom are homeless.

In fact, the polarization of rich and poor, with the unabated retreat of the middle class, is one of the major sources of fearfulness in America. Long-range projections of scarcity and downward mobility, especially for those considered affluent till now, have seriously undermined confidence in the economic future. It is estimated, for example, that the income of U.S. workers has declined 13 percent over the last two decades. One of our recent labor secretaries calls these Americans the "anxious class."

Instead of hopefulness we feel a pervasive sense of discontent, rising out of the fruitless pursuit of the American dream, which for most of us is fast becoming an illusion.[8] Wrestling with accumulation in a culture of compulsive consumerism fueled by dazzling promises of technological advance delivered by sophisticated mass media marketing, many of us are left never truly satisfied and even further in debt than ever. By the turn of the century, an estimated four million Americans are expected to file personal bankruptcy each year. Our own government stares at a five-trillion-dollar debt, projected to be thirteen trillion by the early part of the twenty-first century unless there is a major turnaround.

Paradoxically, despite record prosperity, greater levels of anxiety are being experienced than ever before. Why? Because in the midst of our prosperity we see the future as a time when we may *lose* what we have; we are frozen with the fear that our life of affluence cannot possibly last—that everything is moving in reverse. Yes, we are the anxious class. We are also a nation bereft, in need of messengers of hope.

Deeper Sources of Hopelessness

Our despair rises from much deeper levels too. Social pathologies threaten the very foundation of our families. The divorce rate is at 50 percent, with dramatic rises in child and spousal abuse. Teenage suicide has increased 300 percent since 1940 and is now the second leading cause of death among teenagers. Many other teens are hospitalized for psychiatric treatment, jumping from sixteen thousand in 1980 to nearly three hundred thousand in 1995. Dysfunctional families will produce a new generation of people with negative self-image, pent-up anger, fear of intimacy, and distrust of all authority.

And yet, seven out of ten adults claim that if the traditional family unit falls apart, the stability of American society will collapse.[9] Where can we find hope in such dismal projections?

These national trends are being magnified by "mega-trends" that only increase our sense of foreboding. From the evening news we hear reports of potential mega-famines, pandemics, global plagues, only increased by the multiplication of crowded mega-cities in the Two-Thirds World. Books and movies abound with worse-case scenarios—terrorism, technological piracies, holocausts, economic collapse, even invasions by extraterrestrial beings! Says one European philosopher, "The modern crisis is increased and deepened by the growing sense of urgency, due to the feeling that time is running out."[10]

Returning to our own shores, one of the most disheartening struggles of all is America's current "culture wars." One historian says what is at stake is nothing less than the future of our American democracy.[11] *U.S. News and World Report* writer John Leo claims that the driving theme for his hundreds of weekly columns has been the conviction "that millions of Americans are in shock and mourning at the cultural breakdown we see around us . . . every aspect of Western culture is under assault now."[12] Instead of hope, we find (in the words of Supreme Court nominee Robert Bork) a growing climate of "low morale . . . loss of nerve, which cannot summon the will needed to engage all of these massive problems."[13]

There you have it: a society gripped by fear of the future, a crisis of confidence, and chronic anxiety.[14] We are plagued with pessimism, addicted to despair, infected with contagious cynicism, poisoned with an ingratitude that refuses to acknowledge the countless blessings we enjoy.[15] Sometimes it does feel we should drape across New York harbor not the welcoming words of Miss Liberty to the nations but rather the warning Dante inscribed over his Inferno: "Abandon all hope all ye who enter here."

Never has a nation stood in greater need of messengers of hope. Nothing else but hope from God can bring us out of our disenchantment over the past, our despondency over the present, and our confusion about the future.[16] This familiar tune is being played all through our society. As Cal Thomas observes, "No generation of Americans has ever heard more extravagant promises. Promises of revolution. Promises of Utopia. Promises of ecstasy. Promises of justice."[17] Instead of engendering hope, these shattered promises have left many disillusioned, bitter, and emotionally bankrupt. Even more disheartening, government has channeled literally trillions of tax dollars toward this vast array of crises. In the end, however, it seems all we have done, in most cases, is make things worse. As Chuck Colson says, "We now know that 95% of the things that are ailing our country today, that most of us feel passionately about, are beyond the reach of government."[18]

A Generation of Seekers

The emerging good news, however, is that in the face of social disarray, there is a growing hunger for spiritual reality. "No serious moral conservative doubts the severity of America's cultural crisis. But just when time seems darkest, rays of light may be breaking through, creating a rare moment of opportunity for Christians," writes Chuck Colson.[19] Since spiritual impoverishment is the main ailment of our society, it is not hard for us to conclude that spiritual renewal is our greatest solution. If, in the words of Aleksandr Solzhenitsyn, our culture has been overtaken by "spiritual exhaustion," then this is also a moment when, in the midst of despair, Americans may be actively looking as never before for a message that gives hope—not any hope, but the hope of true spiritual renaissance.[20]

In fact, signs are everywhere that people are asking deeper questions such as, "Isn't there something *more* than this?" and, "Is there something God has to say to us in the midst of it all?" For example, a recent survey among teenagers found that their single greatest concern is the decline in moral and social values, and that 70 percent believe that religion is meant to have a significant impact.[21] Writes a baby buster in *Life after God:* "My secret is that I need God— that I am sick and can no longer make it alone. I need God to help me give, because I no longer seem to be capable of giving; to help me be kind, as I no longer seem capable of kindness; to help me love, as I seem beyond being able to love."[22]

Think for a moment what a consensus of thought about God brought to previous generations of Americans. Not only did it provide the basis of our morality, it was also the basis of our hope. God was someone permanent to hold on to, a way of making sense out of our lives, a source of courage for the future. Currently many Americans, recapturing that vision, are transforming themselves into a "generation of seekers."[23] Like the title of a public television series in 1996, we are increasingly "searching for God in America," and this search could possibly drive the strongest U.S. religious revival we have ever seen.

Newsweek documents that 58 percent of our citizens feel the need to experience spiritual growth and are thus on a quest for spiritual meaning, in pursuit of the truly sacred. Beginning the day with Prozac *and* prayer, many are expecting heaven to help make life livable again. As a matter of fact, many *are* praying (though understandings of prayer widely differ). In a recent survey it was found that 90 percent of Americans pray to God, 61 percent make specific requests, 60 percent do it daily, and nearly 50 percent also listen for and expect answers from God.[24]

These people would probably concur with Shirley Dobson, chairperson of America's National Day of Prayer, that "our national problems are too overwhelming. They are problems of the heart, and only God can change the heart."[25] Looking out over this same landscape, Christian business leader John Beckett, a member of the National Prayer Committee, concludes: "Our hope is in God. Are we desperate enough to believe this? We have so many ideas and techniques. We are so comfortable with responses born out of tradition, out of 'experience.' Abandoning ourselves to Almighty God must become our first impulse . . . we have no other hope."[26]

It is just such a time as this that French Christian philosopher Jacques Ellul wrote about thirty years ago in the book *Hope in Time of Abandonment*. He saw the spiritual crisis looming and predicted it would be a crisis of global proportions. He anticipated that Western societies would increasingly sense that our condition was evidence God had stepped back—that he had, in a sense, "abandoned" us to our own devices until we are ready to acknowledge that our hope is in him exclusively. Ellul's encouraging thesis is irrefutable: When nothing decisive is forthcoming out of all man's institutions, revolutions, and plans, then that puts us back again to the place where we are "waiting for something to happen, the something which will make us alive again. We have no more resource within ourselves."[27] Historically, that something has been revival! That's the hope such a time of abandonment requires, the hope God offers.

Campaigning for Christ

Nationally, then, a large audience is moving into this waiting state of mind. It is an audience especially prepared for the message of hope—a hope centered on Christ, a hope that draws its framework from thousands of biblical promises, a hope that can be unleashed in an outpouring of the Holy Spirit for any generation that opens itself to receive it. With conviction born out of years of desperate longing for God's breakthroughs in his own ministry, J. I. Packer interprets the contemporary drama this way:

> To moderns drowning in hopelessness, disappointed, disillusioned, despairing, emotionally isolated, bitter and aching inside, Bible truth comes as a lifeline, for it is future-oriented and hope-centered throughout . . . the hope that the Scriptures bring us arrests and reverses the drowning experience here and now, generating inward vitality and renewed joy, and banishing forever the sense of having the life choked out of us as the waves break over us . . . the Bible throughout is a book of hope.[28]

A nation drowning in hopelessness? Then we are a people in need of—and being primed for—this message. To expand on the water metaphor, now is clearly the time to flood our land with messengers of hope! I firmly believe the most strategic thing any of us can do for the advancement of Christ's kingdom in this hour is to be a part of making this happen . . . beginning inside the church.

George Barna's *Absolute Confusion* documents that our greatest need in churches called to minister to such a decaying nation is for strong, visionary leadership: "men and women who can envision the better future God wills for his people; who will motivate people to action; who will create intelligent plans for positive change; and who will spearhead the implementation of those plans, for the enduring glory of God."[29] Are you willing to be one of those leaders? Are you willing to campaign throughout the nation for the hope of revival that Christ gives to, in, and through his church?

Consider a recent presidential campaign launched with bold headlines proclaiming, "Hope is back!" The next three months of political maneuvering were all designed to convince the American voter that this candidate's party offered the greatest hope to our nation—a bridge into the twenty-first century. That's the spirit with which political campaigns are waged.

Let's start a similar campaign. On behalf of the Lord Jesus Christ and the agenda of his kingdom, let's bring a revolutionary hope to the American people through a church that is itself already abounding in it. Political strategists see that America needs hope. Without the one true resource to bring it about, without any permanent hope of their own, they make multiple promises to achieve their own purposes. How much more should we, as children of the almighty God, be willing and active in freely, widely, and enthusiastically proclaiming a hope that has already been secured for us by the living Christ himself? God-given revival is the true bridge of hope into a twenty-first century more wonderful and power-filled than any of us can even imagine. Let's say so. Let's be God's agents to help build it.

True, America may be "slouching toward Gomorrah"; there is ample room for brooding pessimism if we allow it. But there is also room for hope, hope that is anchored in the gospel of Christ, hope that is backed by the Word of God. As Judge Bork concludes, "for the immediate future what we probably face is an increasingly vulgar, violent, chaotic, and politicized culture . . . the pessimism of the intellect tells us that Gomorrah is our probable destination. What is left to us is the determination not to accept that fate and the courage to resist it—the optimism of the will."[30]

Across the land, messengers of hope have reached a similar determination. But they've done so with this caveat: We must not and will not accept a church stuck in a pre-revival condition. For them, the courage to resist the spirit of hopelessness so pervasive upon our land rises out of the revealed character, ways, and promises of God in Jesus Christ. To make a difference, they have chosen to proclaim the one message that can transform the future. Contrary to Bork's conclusion, theirs is not simply an "optimism of the will." It is so much more. Theirs is (as Billy Graham told us in the rotunda) a hope for America that arises out of the prospects of spiritual rebirth—personal, corporate, national. We're talking about nothing less than a full-blown spiritual awakening to Christ, and to Christ alone!

Could *you* be one of these messengers of hope? Absolutely.

Descend! descend! Thou gracious God of Heaven!
　　And with Thy glory fill this beauteous fan;
Descend! and let Thy mercy here be giv'n;
　　Descend! and let Thy statutes here obtain.
O, *here,* the mantle of Thy love outspread,
　　And let Thy richest blessings *here* be shed.

Here may the light of holy truth dispel
　　The moral darkness of the human mind,
Defeat the combined power of earth and hell,
　　And achieve all the heart of Christ design'd;
Here let the dews of Christian love distill.
　　And peace divine each faithful bosom fill.

Speak here, great Savior, and the blind will see;
　　The deaf will hear, the dumb will sing Thy praise. . . .

Redeemer! may the cause of missions here,
　　Receive a high, a most exalted place,
And many a herald go from hence to bear
　　The joyful message of redeeming grace. . . .

Here may the heralds of salvation be
A spotless priesthood, and from error free.

Daniel Alexander Payne,
"A Sacred Ode: A Prayer
for the Consecration of a Pulpit" (1866),
taken from *Conversations with God:*
Two Centuries of Prayers by African-Americans

CHAPTER TWO

MESSENGERS OF HOPE, AGENTS OF REVIVAL

Speaking at commencement services for West Virginia University, public television's Mister Rogers left graduates with the words of French philosopher Teilhard de Chardin: "The world tomorrow will belong to those who brought it the greatest hope." That's also the driving conviction of every Messenger of Hope. That's our calling. Now is the time to flood our nation with those who can point us to our greatest hope for tomorrow, the hope of a spiritual awakening to Christ.

The task is not as impossible as it may seem. Africa, for example, has the highest birth rate in the world, with two thousand different culture groups. Many of these groups are locked in tribal wars, with a poverty level that leaves most of its citizens surviving on less than five hundred dollars a year. And yet the church has not retreated! Claiming Africa as the "Continent of the Twenty-First Century," African believers have risen throughout their nations to provide a "wake-up call." Says Tokumboh Adeyemo, general secretary of the Association of Evangelicals: "You have churches vigorously proclaiming a theology of hope across the continent, rather than a theology of pessimism."[1]

Not only in Africa, but within our own nation, the formula of Psalm 68:11 remains. When the Lord activates his word of promised revival, expect the company of those who proclaim it to be great.

Actually, all of God's children were born again to be messengers to somebody, somewhere (Acts 1:8). Here's the question before us in this chapter: Precisely what kind of messenger will I be? Will I be a Messenger of Hope?

Who Are the Messengers?

The Holy Spirit is always *the* "Agent of Revival." No human can create revival. But biblically and historically, God has worked through multitudes of godly men and women to get the church ready for revival by calling Christians into prayer for revival and into holiness of life. Consistently they have been agents used of God to proclaim and promote throughout the church a dynamic vision of Christ-centered renewal. They have been leaders in revival—many who might be considered the least likely candidates—because they have had a message of hope and delivered it.

Those calling for renewal of the church agree that the same is true today: Spiritual leadership, whether pastoral or lay, must be visionary. Our leaders must be full of hope, operating with "conviction, determination, purpose, and a plan." They must lead decisively so the vision they present "completely, clearly, and convincingly enables people to see God's dreams for the church, and to believe in that vision so thoroughly, that the vision becomes their own."[2]

Agents of revival are always infectious because they are visionary. I think of the Los Angeles International Church, housed in the former Queen of Angels Hospital in the inner city. Under the future-oriented leadership of their twenty-something pastor, they've raised up 120 different ministries. Overflowing with hope in God, they even term their church "City of Hope," as they embrace the homeless, unwed mothers, gang members, drug addicts, alcoholics, immigrants, homosexuals, and a whole host of other needy people. Combined ministries reach more than twenty thousand people a week. In everything they do, hundreds are messengers of hope—agents of the very revival for which they pray. Their witness should encourage us all.

Or, consider a messenger of hope from Nigeria. A graduate student at the University of Colorado in the early 1990s, this young man began to invite pastors in Boulder to step out of their frustration, anger, and division, and step in to prayer meetings for revival. Those prayer gatherings not only turned the churches around, but the city as well. The pastors also formed a ministry to the city called "City Vision" that increased the number of messengers of hope. Some, taking up the vision of their Nigerian catalyst, have begun to proclaim the hope of revival in other cities across America.

Anyone can be a Messenger of Hope. I think of my friend Tim. Serving twenty years in a federal penitentiary, he holds an unshakable conviction that God wants to occupy his prison with revival. He has inspired hundreds of inmates to be on fire for Christ with this hope, gathering them in prayer meetings to pray for revival, and in Bible study and discipleship groups to prepare for revival. They've enjoyed initial installments of revival as well, as scores around them have come to Christ. At one point, prison officials decided to house many of the Christians in one wing of the prison so they could live out the message of hope together day by day! It all began with one messenger of hope who could say with Paul that he may be "chained like a criminal. But God's word is not chained" (2 Tim. 2:9).

If it can happen for Tim, it can happen for any of us. Fathers and mothers can be messengers of hope to their children. Bible study leaders can present the message of hope to their small groups, teachers to their Sunday school classes, elders and deacons to their congregations, youth workers to their Bible clubs, ministry leaders to the organizations they guide.

Biblical Messengers

The Bible itself is *full* of messengers of hope. Sometimes their message was one of "foretelling," as they spoke God's vision about what was coming, proclaiming God's promised future in order to transform the status quo. At other times they were passionately "forth-telling," speaking the words of God about the present, but doing it in a way that challenged people to be ready to enter into greater works just ahead. But in either case, *hope* was the bottom-line gift they brought.

Samuel

God shared his heart consistently as Samuel grew up, so that his message would never "fall to the ground," but finally come with power to all of Israel (1 Sam. 3:19–4:1). Remember the day Samuel spoke a message of hope to the Israelites after twenty years of living in defeat under their enemies: "Commit yourselves to the LORD and serve him only, and he will deliver you out of the hand of the Philistines" (1 Sam. 7:3). They hoped. God thundered. The enemies were routed. The tribes were delivered into forty years of peace.

Azariah

Azariah appeared suddenly at the opening of 2 Chronicles 15, an agent of revival for King Asa. His word? "The LORD is with you when you are with him. If you seek him, he will be found by you . . . do not give up, for your work will be rewarded" (2 Chron. 15:2, 7). In turn, Asa became a messenger of hope as he drew the nation into a whole-hearted commitment to seek the Lord together. Azariah and Asa hoped in God, and massive revival came upon them.

Jahaziel

Sent to Jehoshaphat and a nation faced with certain defeat before Moab and Ammon, Jahaziel admonished, "Do not be afraid or discouraged because of this vast army. For the battle is not yours but God's. . . . You will not have to fight this battle. . . . stand firm and see the deliverance the LORD will give you" (2 Chron. 20:15, 17). The king and his people embraced this vision, singing their hope-filled praises to God. The fear of God (his manifested presence) came upon all the kingdoms around them. In confusion, the Ammonites and Moabites annihilated each other. Another awakening unfolded.

Hezekiah

Hezekiah portrayed a true messenger of hope as he summoned a divided nation into revival. His visionary leadership revitalized the priests' devotion to their calling, ignited spiritual ambition in the administrative leaders of the city, and finally mobilized all the citizens into God's presence. "The hand of God was on the people to give them unity of mind" (2 Chron. 30:12), and substantive renewal ensued.

Nehemiah

After years of captivity, a political executive by the name of Nehemiah disseminated hope to a defeated remnant inside the shattered walls of Jerusalem. Returning from Persia in 444 B.C. to become governor of the few who resettled after years of exiled bondage, Nehemiah encouraged the people to lay hold of a fresh vision for their city and to labor with confidence that their enemies could be overthrown. He promised God's testimony could be established once again through Jerusalem before the nations. The people woke up to God and went to work.

Amos

Yes, the Bible vibrates with messengers of hope! People like Amos, a simple farmer, who could say of his own ministry experience, "Surely the Sovereign LORD does nothing without revealing his plan to his servants the prophets. The lion has roared—who will not fear? The Sovereign LORD has spoken—who can but prophesy?" (Amos 3:7–8).

Micah

Micah came from the countryside to proclaim wonderful visions of revival during the reigns of King Jotham, Ahaz, and Hezekiah. He spoke words like, "But as for me, I am filled with power, with the Spirit of the LORD, and with justice and might, to declare to Jacob his transgression and to Israel his sin" (Micah 3:8). These words were followed by prophecies of the temple being raised up before the nations, with

God's law going forth into all the earth as his people regathered to prosper under his glorious dominion forever (see all of Micah 4).

Deborah

Challenged by a national leadership vacuum, Deborah organized an army of willing volunteers by heralding a God who would enable these hope-filled followers to shine "like the sun when it rises in its strength" (Judg. 5:31).

Joel

To a nation overwhelmed by devastating plagues of locust, Joel became an agent of revival. He declared their despair to be a sign of God's judgment on their sin. Then he called them to a "threshold of hope"—to the temple—to seek the face of God together. Joel's promise? God would spare his people and reestablish his witness through them before the nations.

After the first chapter, Joel's primary message is not one of doom and judgment. Nor is it ultimately a call to repentance and brokenness (as essential as that is). Instead, the second half of his book paints a joyous vision. Look at the prospects: The Lord will answer their prayers; he will satisfy them fully. Their land will once again overflow with God's blessings; he will repay them the years that the locusts have eaten. Afterward God will pour out his Spirit on all people, gather all the nations into judgment, and open up a fountain of blessing that causes Judah to be inhabited with the visible presence of the Lord forever.

You know what's amazing about this account in Joel? One of God's promised results of revival was that everyone—even servants—would become prophets like Joel, messengers of hope (Joel 2:28–29). Even a few strong messengers of hope are a sign of early awakening. Messengers don't just precede revival; their existence is evidence that revival has begun!

Habakkuk

According to Habakkuk, as the revelation of God's greater work—to cover the earth with his glory as the waters cover the sea—

becomes "plain," heralds (messengers of hope) will run with it (Hab. 2:2). They will do so confident that the vision will not linger, but that "it will certainly come and will not delay" (Hab. 2:3). Even Habakkuk himself became such a messenger: "LORD, I have heard of your fame; I stand in awe of your deeds, O LORD. Renew them in our day. . . . he enables me to go on the heights" (Hab. 3:2, 19). Interestingly, Habakkuk's book was written to be sung in the temple, and thus to be his ongoing message of hope to all who came to worship (see Hab. 3:19).

Ezekiel

When Ezekiel faced the proverbial valley of dry bones, God told him revival would come for the nation—though it felt lifeless, dry, useless, and hopeless—if Ezekiel would speak to the bones just one bold message: "I will make breath enter you, and you will come to life. . . . They say, 'Our bones are dried up and our hope is gone; we are cut off.'. . . I am going to open your graves and bring you up from them. . . . I will put my Spirit in you and you will live, and I will settle you in your own land" (Ezek. 37:5, 11–14). You know the rest of the story. The Spirit came. The bones drew together. Up rose a mighty army. Revival!

Zechariah

A short time ago a Christian talk show host asked me: "Of all the Bible characters, which one would you most like to be?" For a moment I was caught speechless. Finally, one character loomed before me. I responded, "I would most like to be the prophet Zechariah." The interviewer returned, "For heaven's sake, why?" I'm sure it was not the answer he expected. But my reasoning was quite simple: "His primary role was to bring hope to a very defeated remnant, and to stir them up to rebuild the temple, the place of prayer. He did it by giving them a series of nine major visions, each one sketching what a national revival would look like, each one backed by solid promises from God. What Zechariah did for believers in the sixth century B.C., I would like to do for my own generation. I want to be known as a Christian who bears words of hope—the hope of revival—to awaken churches to Christ who are currently living in fear, defeat, futility, exhaustion."

Isaiah

Of course, when listing messengers of hope, the preeminent Old Testament example is Isaiah. Some of the most glowing descriptions of revival anywhere emerge from the heart of this major prophet. Out of an encounter with God's exaltedness and Isaiah's own sin, God asked if Isaiah would be willing to be an agent of revival. To this Isaiah responded, "Here am I, send me!" (Isa. 6:8). Although his initial mission appeared to be one of judgment (Isa. 6:9–12), Isaiah's ultimate audience was the "holy seed," the remnant starting point for wholesale revival (v. 13).

The promise to him (and to all messengers of hope) was that God would vindicate the words of his servants and "fulfill the predictions of his messengers" (Isa. 44:26). Isaiah was to prepare God's people for extensive spiritual awakening (see chapter 40). As a result, Zion would rise up, clothe itself, shake off its dust, and sit enthroned in the midst of God's glory (52:1–2). Invigorated with this kind of ministry, Isaiah concludes: "How beautiful on the mountains are the feet of those who bring good news, who proclaim peace, who bring good tidings, who proclaim salvation, who say to Zion, 'Your God reigns!' Listen! Your watchmen lift up their voices; together they shout for joy. When the LORD returns to Zion, they will see it with their own eyes" (Isa. 52:7–8). Obviously, he expected messengers like himself to multiply.

Jesus: *The* Messenger of Hope

With such a parade of heralds, it's no surprise the Old Testament closes with Malachi's promise: "See, I will send my messenger, who will prepare the way before me. Then suddenly the Lord you are seeking will come to his temple" (Mal. 3:1). This prophet reassures us that when God manifests his glory, he *himself* will be the messenger who refines his people and enfolds them with healing in his wings (see 3:1–4; 4:2). Of course, Isaiah sounded this promise as well when he spoke of the servant of the Lord, portrayed multiple times as a messenger of hope (see Isa. 11:1–5; 61:1–4).

Then it happened. The Son of God appeared on the scene as a sower of seed, proclaiming the word of the kingdom—a message of hope—everywhere he went (Mark 4:14). The Word had taken flesh! The message was a person (John 1:14). The supreme agent of revival was now among us. How curious that messengers of hope even surrounded his birth—angels delivering good news right and left, Joseph to Mary, Mary to Elizabeth and Elizabeth back, Zechariah to worshipers, shepherds to sleepy Bethlehem, Simeon to Jesus' parents, Anna to those awaiting the redemption of Jerusalem, even Eastern dignitaries to hard-hearted Herod. Surely all this activity was a sign of things to come.

To inaugurate his mission, Jesus reached back to Isaiah 61:1: "The Spirit of the Sovereign LORD is on me, because the LORD has anointed me to preach good news to the poor." He embodied every messenger that preceded him (see Luke 4:18–21). Claimed by Matthew to be the preacher of Isaiah 42 (compare Matt. 12:15–21 with Isa. 42:1–4), Jesus came offering a hope big enough for all nations. Mark actually summarizes Jesus' tidings into three major themes of hope: "The time of great awakening, proclaimed in God's Word, has come. God's sovereign initiative to do this is about to break in upon you. Therefore wrap your whole life around this good news and follow me" (1:14, author's paraphrase).

Other Messengers Follow

Later, as he prepared to leave his mission in the hands of his disciples, Jesus spent his last forty days walking with them in new creation splendor, his own resurrection opening their minds to understand the broad horizons of Scripture. They must grasp how the hope fulfilled in him was to now be unleashed into all the earth (compare Luke 24:45–48 with Acts 1:1–8). Before long, his message was flooding the nation of Israel and beyond. The Spirit of promise came. Messengers of hope went out. Following the day of Pentecost, they were irrepressible. Within just one generation, they helped foster a symphony of spiritual awakenings to Christ throughout the entire Roman Empire!

Preeminent among these messengers was the apostle Paul himself. On two occasions Paul claimed one of his primary gifts was to be a "herald" (1 Tim. 2:7; 2 Tim. 1:11). In Paul's day a herald, sent by a government official, would run into the center square of a town, proclaim vital news meant for the whole community, and then move on to the next neighborhood. In the same way, Paul was bringing to everyone's attention the destiny offered them in the finished work of Christ (2 Tim. 1:10–11), while also helping believers understand the full implications of his message. He proclaimed that Christ was their hope, dwelling in their midst as the full assurance of all the glorious things still to come (Col. 1:24–28). Paul's message was saturated with hope because his message was defined by Christ.

But "heralding" was not just for Paul. One of the primary ministries of the Holy Spirit is to transform *all* of God's people into messengers of hope to be agents of revival. That's why Jesus insisted his disciples wait in Jerusalem until they were clothed with the Spirit. Peter, in his very first message, reached back to employ the words of Joel to explain: "This is what was spoken by the prophet Joel: 'In the last days, God says, I will pour out my Spirit on all people. Your sons and daughters will prophesy, your young men will see visions, your old men will dream dreams. Even on my servants, both men and women, I will pour out my Spirit in those days, and they will prophesy'" (Acts 2:16–18). All of us are to be prophets. All are to be heralds of hope-filled vision. All are to be agents of revival, day in and day out. We may feel weak and inadequate, but God is willing to empower us to spread this message everywhere we go (1 Cor. 2:1–5). Under the leadership of a sevenfold Spirit who ministers throughout the whole earth, God is willing to flood any generation and any nation with messengers of hope (compare Rev. 5:6 with 2:7, 11, 17).

There you have it. *You* can be a Messenger of Hope. How do I know? Because the Bible is filled with messengers of hope of every shape and size. And wherever they are found, they act as agents of revival. Return to our key verse, Psalm 68:11. What ignites this great company of proclaimers? God's promise of revival, which saturates the entire hymn. Promises produce proclaimers. Hope produces heralds. Always has. Always will.

Epochs of Revival

Historians William Strauss and Neil Howe suggest in their provocative look at America's future, *The Fourth Turning,* that as we enter the twenty-first century, a potentially triumphant golden age awaits us, a supreme opportunity to achieve new greatness as a people. The next few years, they claim, are as full of risk as they are of promise. The stakes are high. A decisive moment is before us. Our culture could go either way. But a major religious awakening is possible.[3] In some ways this parallels my thesis in *The Hope at Hand:* "The twenty-first century will be an age of great hope because it will be an age of world revival in the church."[4] There I explore the many reasons we can have confidence that revival is coming, and why this must become our message of hope.

It is not my purpose here to revisit all I say there. Suffice it to say, revival is a *verb.* It is God at work. Revival proves again that where sin increases, God's grace can overcome it (Rom. 5:20). Confronted with a steady spiritual disintegration in our land, we behold a God who wants to deliver us—not in spite of but *because* of our helplessness. Revival seizes every current manifestation of his Spirit to accelerate, intensify, expand, broaden, deepen, extend, and fulfill it to the uttermost. One phrase (based on passages like Isaiah 44:3) frequently used for this in previous Great Awakenings was "the outpouring of the Holy Spirit." Revival encompasses the hope of the extraordinary, divine interventions that pour out on us the "manifest presence of Christ," a phrase for revival coined by the eighteenth-century Puritans.

In early 1905, Denver, Colorado, was rocked by a spiritual awakening to Christ. The *Denver Post* described the revival in a front-page article in these terms:

All Denver was held in a spell under the influence of the power that is not of ourselves, that makes for righteousness. The Spirit of the

Almighty pervaded every nook. The thousands of men and women radiated the Spirit which filled them, and the clear Colorado sunshine was made brighter by the reflective glow of the light of God shining from happy faces. Seldom has such a remarkable sight been witnessed—an entire great city in the midst of a busy weekday, bowing before the throne of heaven and asking and receiving the blessing of the King of the universe.[5]

Do you believe God would want to impact a whole nation like that? Messengers of hope recognize there have been many such epochs of revival and believe God is not only willing and able but *ready* to do it again on a much wider scale.

In all these seasons of revival—whether the Celtic missionary movements of the sixth to eighth centuries, the mendicant movements of the twelfth and thirteenth centuries, the Pietist and Moravian movements of the seventeenth and eighteenth centuries, or the East African revivals at the mid part of this century—one dominant hallmark has been hope-filled preaching. For example, the thesis of historian Iain Murray in *The Puritan Hope* is that a theology of hope undergirded the teaching of God's Word during the first two Great Awakenings in our own nation and sustained those revivals for decades.[6]

That's why I read with interest a recent article in the *Wall Street Journal* by a graduate school professor in business and economics at the University of Chicago. Entitled "The Fourth Great Awakening," it covered nearly a full page. The scholar summarized three Great Awakenings that have impacted our nation since the early 1700s. He then proceeded to explain his contention that America is in the beginnings of a Fourth Great Awakening, and it is our only hope for survival as a nation. He concluded: "The impact of the Fourth Great Awakening will continue to be widespread and massive. In years to come, it will be impossible to understand political and ethical trends as well as economic developments, without understanding the movement centered in enthusiastic religions."[7]

Putting it even more bluntly, George Barna predicted in 1996 that by the early twenty-first century America would experience either anarchy or revival—one or the other—and that only divine intervention could prevent a massive moral and ethical collapse in America.[8]

Hope for Revival Abounds

One hundred leaders met to lead the nation in prayer for revival in a nationally broadcast concert of prayer aired over a thousand radio and television outlets from coast to coast. The next day they joined for an eight-hour discussion on the coming revival, all of which was filmed and produced by the National Prayer Committee for distribution to churches. The title of the video said it all: *Get Ready: Christian Leaders Speak Out on the Coming Revival.*[9] Yes, revival is coming. Messengers of hope are rising up everywhere among us. Listen to them.

"Mired in moral and spiritual crisis, America's only hope is national revival like God has graciously bestowed in the past," says evangelical philosopher Os Guinness.[10] Defining revival as "the refilling of a nation with the glory of the Lord,"[11] he concludes: "Such a revival on the order of the first or second Great Awakenings is inconceivable to many Americans . . . [but] America's future lies unquestionably with the prospects of such a wild card factor."[12]

In a *U.S. News and World Report* article entitled "America Sees Spiritual Awakening," Billy Graham writes on his predictions for 1996 and beyond: "There is much discouragement, despair and negativism in the nation today. . . . there are still hopes to be realized. . . . it is my conviction that we are going to see a great spiritual renewal in America. . . . if we're to be strong as a people, then we must have a strengthening of our moral and spiritual life."[13]

African-American economist Glenn Loury suggests the crisis of racism can only be met through revival in its largest sense. Seeing signs that God has already begun a revival, Loury states in an interview, "I don't rule out [the possibility of a John Wesley–type renewal]. The idea that such a movement can take place is not at all out of the question for me. I don't think it is far-fetched. In fact, I think the circumstances require it."[14]

Such a perspective also dominates the thinking of senior missiologist Ralph Winter, who, pondering the prospects of completing the Great Commission, says, "Our plans cannot even begin to predict or control revival fire. Is it not likely that the God who has often blessed this world with revival in the past will employ that kind of fire again? It has been said that in a true revival, God can do in twenty minutes what might otherwise take twenty years. Are we praying for revival?"[15]

In the mid 1990s, seven thousand youth workers from more than one hundred denominations and ministries gathered for a first-of-its-kind youth leaders' conference under a banner that read, "United for Spiritual Awakening." It was followed by the National Clergy Conference, the largest in church history, bringing together almost forty thousand ministers. Those who attended met with the absolute conviction that we are on the verge of the greatest revolution in the history of the church. In both events I had the privilege of leading a session of prayer for revival. I knew I was looking at a sea of messengers of hope, a groundswell of agents of revival. Expectant. Ready to proclaim the intervention of God's grace in awakening. Ready to multiply other messengers throughout their churches to join them.

Nine Characteristics of the Messengers

So, are *you* ready to become a Messenger of Hope? Anyone can be one. What does such a person look like?

First, writes John Stott, "Every authentic ministry begins with the conviction that we have been called to handle God's Word as its guardians and heralds."[16] In addition, as I've worked with messengers of hope throughout the years across the body of Christ—and as I have sought to be one myself—I've identified nine characteristics that mark the thinking and behavior of those who are ready to share this exciting news of impending revival. Every messenger of hope will likely share these characteristics and convictions.

1. A Messenger of Hope recognizes *Christ* is our message. He is the "hope of glory." We'll look at this more closely in chapter 6, but making him the major issue is our chief task in proclaiming this message of hope.
2. A Messenger of Hope acts in the power of the Holy Spirit, whose major ministry is to take the things of Christ and reveal them to us, especially to show us what is to come (John 16:12–

15). He causes us—and our message—to abound with hope (Rom. 15:13).

3. A Messenger of Hope is marked by a lifestyle of hopefulness. After all, "the medium is the message." Hope must mark how we approach the "living out" of the message of hope. Our daily decisions must constantly be wrapped around the hope of revival, and nothing short of that will do.

4. A Messenger of Hope is a person of prayer. Before he or she speaks that message to others, a Messenger of Hope prays his or her message back to God. I've seen this beautifully illustrated in the Pastor Prayer Summits the last decade, which have brought together tens of thousands of Christians in days of extended prayer over their ministries, their cities, and the nation. Again and again, they have been transformed into messengers of hope because of how God broke through into their hearts as they sought his promises by seeking his face together in prayer.

5. A Messenger of Hope looks at our generation with "superspective." By "superspective" I mean a perspective that includes a vision for the future as God sees it. In his book *The Supremacy of God in Preaching,* John Piper says it well for all messengers of hope: "Good preachers will look out over the wasteland of secular culture and say, 'Behold your God! . . . [who else] will paint for them the landscape of God's grandeur? Who will remind them with tales of wonder that God has triumphed over every foe?? Who will cry out above every crisis, 'Your God reigns!'? . . . If God is not supreme in our preaching, where in this world will the people hear of the supremacy of God?"[17] As a Messenger of Hope, constantly inhabit the great visions and promises of God in his Word. The more you do, the more comprehensive will be your message of hope. But you must also survey the whole world as God sees it. In other places I have called such messengers "world Christians." Your hope must encompass the whole plan of God for all the nations, and you must say so. (See my book *Stand in the Gap.*)

6. A Messenger of Hope serves with genuine compassion for those hungry for hope. A Messenger of Hope realizes that a message of hope (the hope of revival) is one of the greatest gifts

he or she can give to strengthen the life of the church. Like Paul, this person seeks to be both mother and father to those with whom he or she communicates, wanting others to receive the message as if from God (1 Thess. 2:10–13). One of the most compassionate acts of a Messenger of Hope, however, is to keep prodding the hearers: "Does God have more for us than we have yet experienced? Do we need him to respond to us more than ever? Can we ever ask him to do too much?" Compassionate visionaries are even willing to be "irritants," to act with tough love that lays tracks that will help "rip people out of their comfort zones."[18]

7. A Messenger of Hope makes raising others to the task a top priority. A Messenger of Hope is committed to raising up "prisoners of hope," men and women whose lives are captivated by a vision for revival who then begin to act accordingly in their prayers and obedience. In the next chapter, I will discuss more thoroughly this ultimate impact of every message of hope. In looking for such prisoners, agents of revival will focus first on the praying people throughout the body of Christ. They are the ones who have already begun to be captivated by this vision and are more predisposed to labor for revival than others within the body. Rather than being desperate for a message that can hold our audience, Messengers of Hope instead proclaim the message as it is, in search of its true audience. God's praying people are the primary hearers for the message of hope, ready to respond.

8. Messengers of Hope work *smart* not just hard. They seek to be skillful in how they deliver their message. The second half of this book discusses ways for you to be most effective as an agent of revival, reproducing your vision in God's people. By being pragmatic, you can better call your hearers to a specific obedience that allows the message to have its thorough work in their lives.

9. Messengers of Hope, like all servants of Christ, must be ready to sacrifice to fulfill their calling. The price corresponds to the uniquely strategic dimension of being a Messenger of Hope. The biblical record on a multitude of messengers pulls no punches: Prophets pay! (Luke 6:22–23). Henry Blackaby, echo-

ing his *Fresh Encounter: Experiencing God in Revival and Spiritual Awakening,* says it well: "Lord, whatever it costs me, I release my life to you to be a spiritual leader during these times of crisis. Do with me whatever you will. Amen."

We live in a nation desperate for messengers of hope. The greatest need of the hour is to flood our nation with agents of revival. Every Christian is a messenger of something, to someone. Is God calling you to be a Messenger of Hope? If so, let me encourage you with words of John Calvin given to me by European spiritual leaders gathered in Vienna, Austria, to outline the future of Christ's kingdom on the continent:

Whatever resistance we see today offered by almost all the world to the progress of the truth, we must not doubt that our Lord will come at last to break through all of the undertakings of men and make a passage for His Word. Let us hope boldly, then, more than we can understand; He will still surpass our opinion and our hope.[19]

O, MY God! in all my dangers, temporal and spiritual, I will hope in thee who art Almighty power, and therefore able to relieve me; who are infinite goodness, and therefore ready and willing to assist me.

O, precious blood of my dear Redeemer! O, gaping wounds of my crucified Savior! Who can contemplate the sufferings of God incarnate, and not raise his hope, and not put his trust in Him? . . . succored or abandoned by the good things of this life, I will always hope in thee, O, my chiefest, infinite good . . .

Blessed hope! be thou my chief delight in life, and then I shall be steadfast and immovable, always abounding in the work of the Lord.

Richard Allen,
"A Prayer for Hope" (1787–1830),
taken from *Conversations with God:
Two Centuries of Prayers by African-Americans*

CHAPTER THREE

TURN FELLOW CHRISTIANS INTO PRISONERS OF HOPE

A little girl snuggled with her grandmother as they read from a child's Bible. After three or four stories, the grandmother was ready to stop and get her granddaughter ready for bed. But the little girl kept insisting she read another, then another, and still another. Finally, in exasperation, the grandmother said, "Why do you want to hear so many all of a sudden?" Her granddaughter responded, "Because, Grandma . . . I just realized you never know what God is going to do next!"

How is it with you? Is your Christian life filled with a similar atmosphere of suspense? Do you find yourself standing on tiptoe, as it were, alive with anticipation? Are you waiting daily to see what God is bringing around the corner as he parades before you fresh demonstrations of renewal, enticing you with preparations for fuller revival in his church? In other words, are you a prisoner of hope?[1]

When our family moved to the metro New York area in the early 1990s, we did it for one major reason. During previous trips to the city in my work with the prayer movement there, I had met thousands living with a conviction that God wanted to awaken his church in that city in answer to their prayers. Everything told me that God would not disappoint them; an "urban Pentecost" was in the offing.[2] I wanted us to be near enough to the action so we could see it, experience it, and learn from it firsthand. Since then, the prayer movement has greatly increased, including an ongoing twenty-four-hour prayer vigil by over a hundred churches. The suspense mounts! The hope of revival pervades every part of the body of Christ. I call these people "prisoners of hope." And to every messenger of hope in New York, these revival-captivated believers are "our hope, our joy, or the crown in which we will glory in the presence of our Lord Jesus when he comes"(1 Thess. 2:19).

Are there people like that in your life? People who have grasped on to the hope for revival and live out each day with the confidence and expectation that God is about to "surprise" us spectacularly? Do you want there to be more people like that? Essentially, that is your mission as a Messenger of Hope.

In *The Hope at Hand* I define prisoners of hope as pacesetters for world revival. I explain practical ways to uncover, mobilize, and even multiply such people. Now in this companion volume, I want to speak specifically on how to activate such pacesetters through the *message* we share. They may be sitting around our dinner table, attending our home Bible study group, or scattered throughout the Sunday morning congregation. In a very real sense, they actually form the first phase of the revival we've come to tell them about.

Why Call Them Prisoners?

The phrase "prisoners of hope" was first introduced to me by one of the leading Black Christian pastors in South Africa. Within the spiritual ferment of South Africa, he witnessed repeatedly how seemingly ordinary Christians made a tremendous difference for the healing of his nation. Even in cities like Soweto, they labored for a hope that was kingdom-sized in its dimensions, a compelling vision of God that would not let them go. It was their daily passion. As a result, they transformed history.

Certainly *prisoner* is a good word for such people. Have you ever watched *Court TV* on the cable system? *Court TV* brings America face to face with some of the best-known prisoners in our land. In the courtroom as they stand and face the camera, the accused appear to be as free as anybody else. But in truth, they are not their own. Outside the courtroom they are completely at the disposal of the penal system. Decisions about what they eat, how they dress, and where they sleep are controlled by forces beyond themselves. On the screen they may look like you or me. But in their hearts they are preoccupied and controlled by a totally different agenda.

The same should be said of every Christian. Zechariah describes it: "As for you, because of the blood of my covenant with you, I will free your prisoners from the waterless pit. Return to your fortress, O prisoners of hope; even now I announce that I will restore twice as much to you" (Zech. 9:11–12). Because of Christ's finished work for us, God is forever in the business of transforming prisoners of "waterless pits" (have you experienced any "pits" lately?) into prisoners of hope. Not just any kind of hope either. In this context, Zechariah is talking about nothing less than the supreme hope of personal and worldwide *revival*. Look at some of his preceding words: "See, your king comes to you, righteous and having salvation. . . . He will proclaim peace to the nations. His rule will extend from sea to sea and from the River to the ends of the earth" (Zech. 9:9–10).

And how are such prisoners of hope created? In one simple phrase God tells us: "Even now I *announce* that I will restore twice as much to you" (Zech. 9:12, emphasis added). That's how it happens! That's what happens to others when we are effective Messengers of Hope.

Dying to Be Captured with Hope

Without question the people who need our message are, more often than not, bound up in "waterless pits." In his book *Why Preach? Why Listen?*, Yale professor William Muehl writes: "It is instructive, if somewhat dismaying, to realize how many of the men and women in the pews almost did not come to church that morning. And that in all possibility most of them feel that they are there under false pretenses, that everyone around them feels more confidently Christian than they do themselves."[3] Does that sound like the people who sit around you during Sunday worship? You'd be amazed!

William Hendricks's book *Exit Interviews* tells us there are reasonable explanations why many are leaving the church today.[4] Most could be summarized, however, in one word—*disillusionment.* "Disillusionment with claims made and not kept in personal relationships, stipulations about the Christian gospel that could not be substantiated, suffocating boredom in programs that demanded much but delivered little, and feelings of being marginalized when there were struggles with doubt or with life patterns and bondages from the past. And that's just the beginning." That's how Gordon MacDonald reports Hendricks's findings.[5] What do you think you would discover if you interviewed those you see on a Sunday? Are they prisoners of hope? Or are they an "exit" waiting to happen?

Christian missiologists observe that inner-city churches are often overwhelmed with a spirit of hopelessness, drained by the massive urban challenges around them. But suburban churches also deal with debilitated disciples, "a generation that is discouraged, depressed, tired, lonely, and feeling guilty."[6] There are waterless pits there, too, despite sociological differences.

Furthermore, recent surveys have indicated that evangelicals, in general, are prone to see a less promising future than many other segments of our society.[7] In addition, the people in the pews have a less rosy view of God's work in the body than even the pastor does.[8] You don't have to look long to conclude that churches are often "in a defensive crouch against the power of secular individualism and the agenda of the modern world."[9] One leader bravely raises the question whether Christians are actually *destroying* America due to an impoverished faith in the holy truth that God can use us to restore our decaying culture. Our own endless inner struggle with issues like selfishness and racism have suffocated what little hope we may have had, or may have offered.[10] If we are prisoners to anything, it is survival, not revival.

In other writings, I have suggested many can be trapped in "boxes of pea-sized Christianity" (another term for Zechariah's "waterless pits").[11] We harbor an atmosphere of unbelief, falsely concluding that the level of Christianity we now experience is all God has for us until Jesus comes again. Ours is a predisposition toward the status quo (survival, not revival).[12] How else can you explain that over 90 percent of Christian resources are consumed by Christians on themselves?[13] We lack a passion for revival because we have attempted to make life comfortable without it. We've convinced ourselves to settle for a spiritual shortfall. It's no surprise that in a recent survey, 76 percent of pastors listed as their most pressing priority to motivate their people to pursue spiritual growth, and to motivate the laity to engage in meaningful ministry.[14]

Identifying other waterless pits within a very different arena, the president of the Evangelical Fellowship of Mission Agencies wrote a courageous plea to U.S. mission executives. Without a massive transformation in the U.S. missionary enterprise, it's over, he said. Apart from a dynamic movement of God's Spirit in a true spiritual awakening that ignites people with holy passion for world evangelization, the missionary agencies in North America could, "in the not too distant future, appear analogous to an abandoned ship buried by the tides on a sandy seashore with only its weather-beaten ribs as visible testimony to far better and more useful days."[15]

Prayer versus Pits

There is one great exception to the map of desert places we might survey. A prayer movement has been expanding and accelerating in every part of the body of Christ. This nationwide (and global) manifestation of concerted prayer—expressed in small groups, prayer summits, concerts of prayer, massive city-wide gatherings, national days of prayer and fasting, stadium rallies, and millions of youth united on their high school and college campuses—consists of an army of prisoners of hope! Their heart-level transformation has come about as a result, in part, of *how* they have prayed their vision for revival. But above all, they are an answer to their own prayers. There are literally millions of them throughout our nation. They are a signal that God intends to raise up many more.

I think, for example, of the hundreds of thousands who every year march, sing, and pray in the streets of our cities in what are known as "Marches for Jesus." Sometimes these prisoners of hope—filled with bold hope for revival in their communities—sing a world-renowned contemporary revival prayer that concludes with this chorus: "Shine, Jesus, shine, fill this land with the Father's glory. Blaze, Spirit, blaze, set our hearts on fire. Flow, river, flow, flood the nations with grace and mercy. Send forth your Word, Lord, and let there be light."[16] This is the essence of the message that is capturing believers everywhere.

Recently I traveled to Purdue University, where I spent an evening with four thousand teenagers, seventh through twelfth grades, discussing the message of hope and concluding with a two-hour concert of prayer. Were they tracking with me? Absolutely, right from the very beginning. I couldn't get them to stop praying—and it was already 10:00 P.M.! I've experienced this with countless other teens in similar gatherings. Prisoners of hope! They can appear at any age. They believe God is the key to their future, and they say so.[17]

On another front, I recall five thousand adults throughout the Pacific Northwest who, in 1995, signed a covenant to pray *every day* for revival, until revival comes. Today they are joined by multitudes of others across the land assembling in fasting and prayer convocations, willing to set aside all meals for days at a time because they are filled with hope in what God is about to do. Certainly the Promise Keepers laymen's movement contains ranks of such prisoners. Gathering by the millions, whether in stadiums or on the Mall in Washington, D.C., they are (as one gathering in D.C. recently called itself) Christians willing to "stand in the gap," by prayer most of all. Why? Because they know that revival is the only hope for our nation. Further, they are convinced that revival is coming.

A similar movement of women that started in Houston said it all by the name they gave themselves—Promise *Reapers.* After all, prisoners of hope are primary beneficiaries—the reapers—of all their prayers and all of God's promises, not only as he revives them and their churches, but also as he brings spiritual awakening to the whole nation.

It's no coincidence that Zechariah's discussion of prisoners of hope in chapter 9 is preceded by the final verses of chapter 8, which (as I detail in *Concerts of Prayer*) describe city-wide and nationwide prayer movements that are seeking the face of God.[18] Zechariah concludes with a summary of the awakening that springs from the movement: "In those days ten men from all languages and nations will take firm hold of one Jew [one of the praying people] by the hem of his robe and say, 'Let us go with you, because we have heard that

God is with you'" (Zech. 8:23). That hope—nations acknowledging the manifest presence of God among his people—is centered on the coming King (Zech. 9:9). He mobilizes parched and barren believers to lead them home (9:11–12). Therefore, God announces that he will restore to them twice as much as they've lost in their pits of despair. The message of hope goes forth: God will answer this mighty prayer movement with extraordinary wonders for the sake of all peoples (vv. 10, 13–17). The only response required is to surrender to his vision and to wrap their lives around nothing less.

Created by God

If you want to be a Messenger of Hope, your major assignment is to announce your vision for revival in such a way that others are conquered by it, gratefully, and brought into the victory procession. Are you working to take others captive? Are you asking God to give you prisoners of hope?

As you'll see from the second half of this book, the very way you deliver your message will multiply prisoners in simple, natural ways. But for your encouragement, let me hasten to add, prisoners of hope are created by God. Just as Jesus' fearless words, "Lazarus, come out" (John 11:43), produced deliverance out of death, so prisoners of hope are sovereignly raised up by the life-giving Spirit. He himself transforms the Word of God in our mouths into a compelling message of resurrection proportions. Speaking of faith (and faith is the evidence of things hoped for, so that hope must always precede faith, as we know from Hebrews 11:6), John Calvin writes:

> If we honestly consider within ourselves how much our thought is blind to the heavenly secrets of God and how greatly our heart distrusts all things, we shall not doubt that faith [and thus hope] greatly surpasses all the power of our nature, and that faith is a unique and precious gift of God.[19]

You cannot produce prisoners of hope, but God can! What he needs is faithful agents through whom he can get the job done.

When you properly deliver the message of hope, the Spirit will unleash two immediate responses in your hearers: (1) *Holy desper-*

ation. They will conclude from God's Word that the hope of revival he offers is too wonderful for them to produce themselves. The message will always highlight how helpless and hopeless we sinners are. It will contrast our current condition against the glorious promises God waits to fulfill within us. It will make us restless to climb out of our waterless pits. (2) *Holy anticipation.* Based on the same message, your hearers will conclude that God's promised revival is too wonderful for them to live without any longer. It will fill them with spiritual ambition—not only restlessness to get out of the pits, but also eagerness to move into the fuller dimensions of kingdom life that await us in a God-given awakening to Christ.

Thus, with a hope before them that is too wonderful to personally produce but too wonderful to live without, they will be conquered by the unparalleled hope you herald. This magnificent obsession, born of desperation and anticipation, is a chief hallmark of all prisoners of hope.

The Hope at Hand gives a whole chapter to analyzing prisoners of hope. There, however, I call them "the determined people."[20] Determined they are! The Bible describes them as those who "wait" on God to intervene, or who "watch" for his work of renewal. Let's dub them "Wait-Watchers!" Similar to "Weight-Watchers," their vision of how beautiful things could become makes them determined to set aside all substitutes, to sacrifice whatever it takes to see that vision come to pass.

Exploring biblical hope, Jacques Ellul cautions those who wait on God that they are not engaged in an empty, passive, hollow, drowsy kind of relationship with him. "The waiting is 100,000 times more difficult than action. It demands much more of the person.... Waiting is decisive.... The promise is fulfilled every time in connection with the person who bet his whole life on that promise, that is, in the expectation of its fulfillment."[21]

Seven Steps to Watch For

In conclusion, as you seek to turn fellow Christians into prisoners of hope—Wait-Watchers—with your message of the hope of revival, expect these seven steps to be a part of the transformation you'll see in those who are ready to receive the message you bring.

1. *Awake*—God speaks to the hearers through your message, stirs up faith, and makes them alive with new hope in Christ for renewal and revival.
2. *Agree*—They find others who share that same hope and who are willing to join them in pursuing God's promise of revival.
3. *Ask*—On the basis of the hope revealed to them through your message, they first of all communicate with God about this in prayer, especially in united prayer with other prisoners.
4. *Act*—They also couple their prayers with appropriate daily obedience that prepares them for a greater work, as God pours out his Spirit in a fresh awakening to Christ in answer to their prayers.
5. *Await*—They remain expectant, always watching for the answers, keeping one another encouraged in hope, and unwilling to cease praying or preparing until full revival comes.
6. *Accept*—Furthermore, when they are able to identify preliminary answers to their prayers—first installments of renewal—they receive this with celebration, and give further obedience as appropriate. Thus, every step in the fulfillment of the hope leads them to praise God more and to seek him for even greater demonstrations of his faithfulness and power in the next step.
7. *Acclaim*—They themselves will begin to share this message of hope with those around them, so that prisoners of hope ultimately become Messengers of Hope, who in turn transform fellow Christians into prisoners of hope.

In the second half of this book, I want to share with you practical ways to capture prisoners of hope with your message of hope, in line with these seven steps. But for now, the more important question before you as a potential messenger is this: Do I have the confidence about God-given awakening needed to take fellow Christians captive? Are my convictions solid enough to sustain me in the battle as an agent of revival? Can I persist in my role as Christ's herald even when it feels like the hope grows dim? Will I keep at it into the twenty-first century, if need be? The next chapter helps you find that confidence. For without confidence, no messenger can survive.

Lord, help me to hold out,
Lord, help me to hold out,
Lord, help me to hold out
     until my change comes.

My way may not be easy
You did not say that it would be.
But if it gets dark,
I can't see my way,
You told me to put my trust in Thee,
     that's why I'm asking You.

Lord, help me to hold out,
Lord, help me to hold out,
Lord, help me to hold out
     until my change comes.

Lord, help me to hold out!
Lord, help me to hold out!
Lord, help me to hold out!
Lord, help me to hold out!
Lord, help me to hold out!
Lord, help me to hold out!

I believe that I can hold out!
I believe that I can hold out!
I believe that I can hold out!
     until my change comes.

James Cleveland,
"Lord, Help Me to Hold Out" (1974),
taken from *Conversations with God:
Two Centuries of Prayers by African-Americans*

CHAPTER FOUR

THE CONFIDENCE TO BE A MESSENGER OF HOPE

A survey taken by International Urban Associates asked ministers of inner-city churches: "When have you most felt like quitting on the city, and why have you stayed?" The answers were revealing. Seventy-four percent said they did not resign because it was God's call for them to be there. Of course that's good. But only 10 percent responded that they were sticking it out because of "the potential of great things happening."[1] In other words, motivation for ministry sprang not so much out of their confidence that God would renew his work among them, but rather from a resigned obedience to him even when it was bad enough to quit. Is that really God's best for us?

Contrast the perspective of Bolivian pastor Julio Ruibal, whose devotion to his city of Cali, Columbia, and his ministry of calling for prayer and revival led to his assassination in December 1995. Ruibal and his wife, Ruth, had served Christ in Cali since 1978; they focused constantly on revival for the city. A year or so before his murder, Ruibal was instrumental in initiating all-night prayer and fasting sessions, gathering tens of thousands together in soccer stadiums, seeking God for the overthrow of the illegal drug trafficking out of Cali. The drug cartel was so threatened by this prayer movement—and by Ruibal's hope-filled vision for righteousness in their streets—

that they were left with no other option but to kill him. They gunned him down while he was walking into his church one morning.

Ruibal persisted as a messenger of hope because of his absolute confidence in the promises of God for revival. A day before his death, he told his wife, "We have spent the last seventeen years laying a foundation that is solid. Now is the time for the move of God, and it will be seen. It will shake this whole nation until its history is changed by the gospel."[2]

Do you have the confidence it takes to be a Messenger of Hope?

Will God Show Up?

When you teach the Scriptures to your family, in your church, or in a local Bible study group, do you really expect anything to happen? I'm not asking if you teach *about* God. I'm asking if you actually expect God himself to show up? Isaiah 55:11 tells us that God's Word never returns empty, that it always accomplishes the vision to which it points. Those who hear it will go forth in joy, as they watch mountains break forth with singing before them (Isa. 55:12).

The question isn't whether or not you have confidence about God's promises of revival, the impact of revival, or even the need of revival. The question is do you believe in the *nearness* of revival— that God is not only willing and able but *ready* to fulfill his promises for revival? Do you believe God is going to show up soon?

A world-renowned pastor said it this way: "Revivals are among the charter rights of the church. They are the evidences of its divinity, the tokens of God's presence, the witness of his power. The frequency and power of these extraordinary seasons of grace are the tests and preservers of the vital force in the church. The church which is not visited by these seasons is sterile . . . such churches may have all the show and parade of life, but it is only a painted life."[3] Do you believe revival is the right of the people to whom you speak about our hope in Christ?

One of the most committed Christian leaders on Capitol Hill remarked to me one day that occasionally he will walk up to a congressman and announce, "There's another great spiritual awakening coming to America. And *you* are going to be a part of it!" I'm sure that leaves them thinking, but he's right. If awakening is coming to this nation, everybody will be affected by it in one way or another, including those in Congress. Do you share his kind of conviction? Do you believe awakening is coming? Would you be willing to stand before your family or the people in your church next Sunday morning and say, "There's another great awakening coming, and *you* will be a part of it!"?

Cautious or Courageous?

Many of us who minister struggle at times with a tentative spirit, an unwillingness to fully trust God's Word. We are suspicious that things will not really turn out as God says they will. Though we may not own it publicly, within our hearts we harbor reservations about the hope of revival: *I'll believe it when I see it.* So many times we've had other hopes—lesser hopes—dashed to the ground, and we're not willing to risk such confidence again.[4]

The spiritual leaders in Malachi's day suffered the same undertow of skepticism. "You have wearied the LORD with your words. 'How have we wearied him?' you ask. By saying, 'All who do evil are good in the eyes of the LORD, and he is pleased with them' or 'Where is the God of justice?' . . . You have said, 'It is futile to serve God. What did we gain by carrying out his requirements and going about like mourners before the LORD Almighty? But now we call the arrogant blessed. Certainly the evildoers prosper, and even those who challenge God escape'" (Mal. 2:17; 3:14–15).

Listening to tens of thousands of pastors over the years and reflecting over my own years as a pastor, I know many struggle at times with these same questions: Where is the God of justice? What good does it do to put our lives on the line and believe his Word? Why does he not show up? Why does he not fulfill his promises the way he said he would?

This tentativeness toward God is a major reason why pastor tenure in American local churches is in decline, reflecting high levels of frustration and stress.[5] A recent survey found that 40 percent of ministers have seriously entertained thoughts of quitting the ministry. And it's not just pastors either—mission leaders point out that to counter defection from the missionary cause, one of the greatest needs of the whole enterprise is to protect missionaries' spirits from despair, discouragement, and doubt.[6]

Such fears and doubts plague anyone who desires to be a Messenger of Hope. Plain and simple, it's costly to be a Messenger of Hope, especially if you intend to take others as prisoners of hope. That takes raw courage. As Lewis Smedes observes, "I have come to believe that the only workable response to unfair pain is hope. Hope for what? Hope for the time when pointless and unfair suffering no longer happens . . . hope becomes a kind of courage—courage to trust God with our hopes."[7] Has God given you a reason to hope for revival? Can you find the courage, in the face of all your own pain and disappointments, to trust God with your hopes, no matter what? What is your CQ—your confidence quotient? Or better still—your courage quotient?

Think of Ezekiel standing before a valley of dry, bleached, disconnected, lifeless, helpless, hopeless bones. What did God say to Ezekiel? Essentially he said, "Speak with confidence a message that flies right in the face of what you see: Tell them, 'You will live again'" (see Ezek. 37:1–14). He did *not* say (as we often do in similar situations): "Tell them here's a list of ten practical steps you can take to help you live again." Nor did he say, "Scold them and ask them: 'How come you're not living the way you should?'" Instead, Ezekiel's one responsibility was to speak to the bones the hope of revival, to declare resurrection in the midst of a valley of death. And to speak it with confidence—as if it were as good as done. When you look into the eyes of those to whom God has sent you as his messenger, do you see helplessness, lifelessness, dryness? If so, God wants to give you the confidence and the courage to speak up for the hope of revival anyway. And then to watch what happens!

In 1996, the Promise Keepers organization gathered together the largest clergy conference in history to look at the call of God for spiritual leaders to labor in unity for revival in our nation. The theme of the conference was "Fan the Flame," taken from 2 Timothy 1:6: "Fan into flame the gift of God, which is in you." Paul continues in verse 7, "For God did not give us a spirit of timidity, but a spirit of power, of love and of self-discipline." Be done with timidity, Paul says.

Embrace the confidence to which every Messenger of Hope is called. God expects you yourself to put fire in your ministry.

In 1830, speaking to a graduating class of seminarians, Dr. Ebenezer Porter, founder of Andover Seminary, gave a series of lectures on revival based on firsthand observations throughout much of the Second Great Awakening in the late 1700s to early 1800s. He concluded his teachings with this appeal:

> In modes of preaching and conducting revivals, I would by all means advise you to avoid that hesitating and paralyzing apprehension which leads a minister to be so much afraid of being wrong as to do nothing. Under God, the ministers of the nineteenth century [and the twenty-first century as well!] have a mighty work to accomplish. Our own vast country is to be brought under the influence of the gospel. The wide world is to be evangelized. The day of slumber is past. The sacramental hosts of God's elect are marshaled in arms and wait for ministers to lead them on to victory. Gird on your armor, then, soldiers of the Cross! . . . Stubborn hearts, in numbers unexampled, will bow before the all-subduing influences of his Spirit.[8]

That's the call Paul set before Timothy as well: Don't hesitate! Don't be paralyzed by apprehension. Don't be so afraid you might be found wrong that you do absolutely nothing. The time has come for battle. Our weapon, the message of hope. If we speak it, the Spirit of God will bring about "the all-subduing influences" of genuine awakening to Christ.

When God Inflamed My Confidence

Let me tell you how God delivered me. About fifteen years ago, I had entered into a dark night of the soul, a time of real crisis in ministry. It had little to do with outward circumstances. God was simply stripping me bare on the inside, showing me who I really was; he brought me to the conclusion that I was totally unqualified to remain in ministry. However, a turnaround finally came for me. I can still remember the exact hour as I sat in the living room of our home. It was almost midnight. I knew this because the grandfather clock in the corner continued to chime out the quarter hours as the evening progressed. I'd reached the point—have you been there?—where I had prayed every prayer I knew to pray, shed every tear, and was now a heap of utter brokenness. Silence.

In that moment, when I truly had no hope left for myself or my ministry, God reminded me of 2 Corinthians 1:8–11. Cautiously I turned to it. There I discovered Paul describing the same despairing condition I felt—but about himself! This great apostle experienced such pressure that he was convinced he could not endure it any longer, that he was about to die. His whole being, he wrote, was under a sentence of death. Yet he went on to say that the chief reason God took him into a hole of helplessness was to produce in him a whole new confidence toward God. In fact, he said he *needed* this conflict in order to learn—and how amazing that Paul still had to learn this!—not to rely on himself or to hope in himself, but to put his hope in God who is able to (and must) raise the dead. As a result, God delivered Paul into fresh enthusiasm for ministry, coupled with bold confidence in God's resurrection power. He preached Christ with new understanding wherever he went. He was more a messenger of hope than ever before.

I looked up from the page. Midnight was at hand. Then it was as if God summarized Paul's breakthrough into one sentence that has stayed with me ever since. It is the compass of my service to Christ: "You are right, David, you have no ministry, and you will never have a ministry, unless I raise it from the dead day, by day, by day."

As the years have passed, I've learned that having hope in a God who daily rescues my own ministry from defeat gives me abounding hope in what he can do to raise his church out of the grave, daily, by a fresh outpouring of grace. That's one reason I spread the hope of revival with great confidence. I've had firsthand experience of what I proclaim!

Six Constraints on Confidence

As we attempt to build our confidence in God's ability to act, let's look at the major culprits that rob us of confidence about our message of hope—barriers faced by both clergy and laypeople. In a sense, this list is autobiographical, since I speak from the experience of my own "waterless pits."

1. Ignorance of the Ways of God

Many of us live in a theological vacuum. We are often ignorant of the ways and promises of God relating to revival, or we may underestimate the level of spiritual jeopardy faced by the church that makes revival our only hope. Again, we may ignore the magnitude of the cosmic battle around us that requires reinforcements from God. Many of us have meager facts on what God has done in the past in revival, let alone what he is doing right now. We hear few reports on the preliminary signs and first stages of a coming awakening, although they are already unfolding in the many parts of the church worldwide. Inside boxes of pea-sized Christianity, hope may be no bigger than what relates to our personal struggles, our church traditions, or the limited concerns of our own community of like-minded Christians. Essentially, hope suffocates.

2. Sorrows of Our Own Souls

Why do Christians lose hope? Many sorrows seem to snatch it away: A marriage that has gone sour. Church traditions and programs that squeeze out our dreams. The loss of a job, kids that have left the faith, catastrophic illness. The pain of betrayal. Or, maybe it's our brokenheartedness over the unrelenting spiritual demise of our nation. Whatever circumstances we face, Messengers of Hope must be honest about the sorrows in our souls and how these sorrows impact our confidence about a larger work of God in revival.

The greatest sorrows, of course, are our own sins, which grieve the Holy Spirit (who is the source of all hope and confidence), and cause us to grieve as well. We feel defeated, overwhelmed by our own rebellion and ungodly ways. The most important first step toward regaining confidence, therefore, may be for you to come before the Lord in brokenness and repentance for the sin in your life and to quit grieving God any longer. Paul tells us that godly sorrow brings about repentance and produces in us earnestness, longing, and readiness to get on with the work of God (2 Cor. 7:10–11). The right kind of sorrow delivers us from despair and establishes us in ambitious hope.

3. *Disappointments over Past Ministries*

It's hard to believe in a future revival if our past is plagued with evidences of what *appear* to be times when God failed to come through in ways he promised. We may experience this on a macro level as we watch secularism's steady eroding of our society in spite of all the church attempts to do for Christ. Or maybe it's the prospects of missionary implosion, as 95 percent of the world's population increase over the next fifty years will be in the poorest, least evangelized regions of the world. Faced with such scenarios, we ask the questions: Where has God been in the midst of all of this? How could he allow this to happen?

Closer to home, periodic failures also mock our service to Christ. Writing about the ten most powerful trends facing the church, Leith Anderson sees many pastors under such pressure to produce, to meet unreasonable expectations from their congregations, and to satisfy multiple agendas that "involuntary clergy terminations are at record high levels already and may increase."[9] In point of fact, 22.8 percent of pastors have been forced out of their pastorates at least once—a third of these more than once.

The disappointments that you, as a Messenger of Hope, wrestle with may not be as blatant as this. But most of us have a fairly vivid list of experiences that, from all outward appearances, makes it seem as if God simply failed to produce for us at the level we anticipated; we may even have proclaimed our disappointment to others. Eventually, disappointments lead to frustrations. Frustrations can often lead to an *unholy* desperation that, allowed to continue, may foster a hardness of heart toward God. Unfortunately, most of us have no way to debrief our unraveling of confidence with anyone else. To even speak of such things might make us appear to be questioning the character of God. So we bury our disappointments deep inside us. Eventually, we have little or no ambition left to share a compelling vision of future revival that awakens fellow Christians with great expectations.

4. *Weariness in the Midst of Current Ministries*

In the midst of our frenetic schedules, filled date books, and overwhelmingly busy lives, we may find ourselves on the brink of physical and spiritual exhaustion. Dedicated Christians are often forced to be "chaplains to the rat race,"[10] running rescue operations, helping believers to focus simply on survival—not revival. Many may attempt important work for Christ. But we end up with compassion fatigue, a numbness to any hope of further transformation for our families or our churches or our communities. Concluding that we can make little difference with our own energies, abilities, and ingenuity, we are ready to give up in the face of overwhelming odds. We're certainly not ready to preach to others about a God who wants to do *more* for us. Who needs more of anything right now? We long for *less!*

In a recent survey of pastors conducted by the Evangelistic Association of New England, two-thirds of respondents said that their congregations were not thinking about the future, that their churches no longer had much impact on society, and that trying to lead hesitant churches to change while remaining faithful to Scriptures was "sapping pastors' spiritual vitality."[11]

Vitality is also sapped by divisiveness stemming from local church issues such as the quality of pastoral care, the methodologies of youth ministries, acceptable worship styles, the employment of spiritual gifts, and the prioritizing of outreach opportunities and funds spent on them. *Leadership* magazine concluded that such conflicting visions of the church's ministry may be the greatest source of exhaustion and termination for any in spiritual leadership, whether formal or informal.[12] The fact is, the very structures in which we seek to be Messengers of Hope can rob us of confidence because they are so entrenched and inflexible, so filled with unrelenting gridlock, that weariness becomes a way of life.

Weariness, ultimately, is a sign that we are in *pre-*revival times. In pre-revival times, Christians frequently look to human leadership to be God because they know so little of him themselves and sense so little of his manifest presence. In the end, it is this "spirit of idolatry," which can only be broken by a fresh outpouring of the Holy Spirit, that has pulled many leaders into spiritual exhaustion. At times the difficulty may be of our own making because we have given in to the "idolatrous" expectations of those we serve. We find ourselves trying to please people who have little hope that

God can meet their needs and little vision of *how* he can do it. Their false expectations turn into our obligations—co-opting us for their own agendas, programs, causes, struggles, and heartaches.

In turn, those who should lead are overtaken with a "siege mentality." They feel victimized by the high expectations laid on them in the face of seemingly intractable problems and depleted resources. When messengers of hope are worn out, there is little confidence or energy to herald a coming revival.

5. Fears about Future Ministries

First is the fear: *God won't!* If we share a hopeful vision of a great work of God, we fear that he might not come through, and we will be left holding the bag—embarrassed, ashamed, discredited. Once that fear dominates, we will not have confidence to remain a Messenger of Hope.

Next comes the fear: *God will!* What if our message is fulfilled and revival comes? We may be uneasy about the supernatural manifestations—fearful of the unfamiliar, of fanaticism, of disorder, of emotionalism. We cringe at the possibility of divine intervention because of the potential sacrifices it may require of us or the increased work it may demand. We may fear loss of clout or personal amenities that currently go with our status as a spiritual leader. We have a vested interest in our ministry reputation, in denominational distinctives, in the rights and privileges of our specific calling. The prospect of losing all this in a spiritual revolution may keep us from the confidence, the desire, and the willingness to proclaim such a message of hope. Our true fear, however, may really be of greater intimacy with God, of being saturated with God's presence, and of having our own sins and failures exposed in the light of revival grace.

Finally, there is the fear: *I can't!* We believe we are not spiritual enough to lead people into the greater work of revival. We are anxious that our hearers will go on ahead without us, that in an awakening we will be left behind.

If any of these fears have taken the upper hand, we will lack the confidence needed to be a real Messenger of Hope.

6. Isolation from Other Messengers of Hope

Cocooning has become a way of life in our culture, more so now with chat rooms on the Internet. We're more self-contained, unattached, and uncommitted to others around us. This isolation is a constant danger for those of us insulated inside the evangelical subculture, on retreat in our "religious ghettos." Hope will never be at home there.

This is doubly debilitating for Messengers of Hope. Many have few others with whom to share their dreams or their pain. They lack a sense of solidarity with other agents of revival within their churches. Unable to locate a friendly forum in which to confess, discuss, or debrief their struggles, there's little healing for the things that undermine confidence. With whom do they confront the five barriers listed above, and so bring themselves into subjection to Christ (2 Cor. 10:4–6)?

Do you have colleagues nearby ready to refill your wellsprings of hope? Like the messenger of hope who wrote Psalm 102 (one of the great passages on revival), we often feel, "I am like a desert owl, like an owl among the ruins. I lie awake; I have become like a bird alone on a roof" (Ps. 102:6–7). God never intended us to survive on our own. Probably the single most important step we can take to overcome other barriers to confidence and to arise as ardent agents of awakening, is to begin to link up with two or three other messengers to whom God has given the same passion.

Hope often comes to us through another person wholly devoted to Christ, whose heart is filled with the promise of revival. The more we connect with one another, the more we can build an abounding hope within each other. That's why the movement toward denominational and racial reconciliation within the church in America is such an encouraging sign. Out of reconciliation, many Messengers of Hope will find each other for the first time—just as I have begun to find radical hope from new friendships with African-American agents of revival.

Seven Confidence Builders

So how does one respond to a crisis of confidence? How can you be transformed into a bold and fearless Messenger of Hope? Recently a leading pastor in our nation wrote me a letter expressing his concern about the level of confidence with which I speak on the coming revival. He said in part, "The question I have is whether you believe you have a genuine prophecy from the Lord that such a revival is coming, or whether this is simply a high hope, or whether it is a logical deduction from the evidence?" Good question. To him I responded:

> Let me reassure you that I do *not* have nor claim to have a specific prophecy, or an angelic word outside of Scripture regarding a coming revival. *Yes,* I do have a great deal of confidence (along with thousands of other Christian leaders around the world) that a great revival is in the offing. That confidence is shaped by Scripture, and in the full spirit and teachings of Scripture on revival. I believe it is a confidence not different from that held by the "patron saint" of the First Great Awakening, Jonathan Edwards.
>
> No, I've had no visions in the night. I can't claim to possess "absolute proof." But I can't imagine being more convinced if God did appear to me in some desert retreat. If you could walk with me through the years I've spent studying Scripture and church history on the topic—and if you could only retrace my travels the past twenty years into all parts of an awakening church worldwide—I'm sure you would be as convinced as I am!
>
> In my book *The Hope at Hand,* I have seven chapters in the center that spell out in detail "Seven Confidence Builders" I believe are irrefutable. When taken together, they give us every reason to pray and to prepare for revival with the confidence that God will not let us be disappointed.[13]

Let me conclude this chapter by summarizing for you here the "Seven Confidence Builders" that I mentioned to my friend. They're like a lawyer's brief, establishing for us and our hearers a reasonable verdict about the hope we proclaim. Peter tells us we should always be ready to do this for any who ask us (1 Peter 3:15).

1. The Decisive Person

God intends for his Son to be at the center of everything—at the end of history and at every step along the way. In revival, God dramatically intervenes to restore Christ's rightful role as Redeemer King among his people and to more fully advance his kingdom, right now, among the nations. Therefore, we can pray and prepare for a coming revival with confidence.

2. The Divine Pattern

God is faithful and consistent in all his ways. He has been pleased to grant times of significant revival throughout generations of his people, both in Scripture and in church history. What he has done before, he is able, willing, and ready to do right now for our generation. Therefore, we can pray and prepare for it with confidence.

3. The Dark Prospects

God loves the world and longs to see his Son exalted among all earth's peoples. But he knows the world is currently facing extraordinary crises and challenges beyond its own resources. Revival in the church, equal to the desperate needs of our time, is the only hope he currently holds out for the world he loves. Therefore, we can pray and prepare for it with confidence.

4. The Disturbing Paralysis

God also sees that the desperate condition of the world is largely due to the church's struggle with its own spiritual powerlessness, brokenness, dullness, and sin. But he intends to bring glory to himself through the church. The only hope for this is for God to heal us corporately of our paralysis and our sin. That healing is called revival. We can pray and prepare for it with confidence.

5. The Dramatic Preparations

The attempts of the contemporary church to fulfill the Great Commission form nothing less than a prelude to revival. God is obviously setting the stage worldwide for a whole new advance of Christ's kingdom. If this is his work of preparation, he will not fail to bring it about. We can seek revival with confidence that it is coming.

6. The Distinctive Praying

God is stirring up his people to pray specifically, increasingly, and persistently for world revival. He will not let us pray in vain. These are his prayers, and he has promised to hear and answer us fully. We can prepare for the answers with confidence.

7. The Determined People

God is galvanizing a host of people worldwide—prisoners of hope—who are convinced that revival is the only hope for the church and for the nations. They are willing to pay any price to prepare the way for God to do it. They form a chief sign of the nearness of an impending spiritual awakening to Christ. In fact, they are the first phase of it. Surely, revival is on top of us. Of this we can be confident.

Connecting with Other Messengers of Hope

Each one of these confidence builders, taken by themselves, is sufficient to recharge us with enough confidence to deliver our message day after day. All of them taken together should give us enough confidence to stand our ground as God's messengers until full revival comes. When we meet together with other Messengers of Hope, this can form a major part of our agenda, both for discussion and prayer. I suggest that you ask God to give you one or two others to meet with regularly in order to do the following together:

> Share the message of hope that is already growing in your heart in anticipation that the more you share, the more it will grow.
>
> Talk about what you see God doing even now (as well as what he has done in the past) to bring forth revival.
>
> Work through the barriers that rob each of you of confidence; talk honestly about your struggles.

Report on one another's ministry of hope, describing specifically the challenges you face in the coming week or month.

Focus on building confidence in each other as you reflect over one or more of the seven confidence builders.

Study Scripture passages on the hope of revival and brainstorm together on how you might share that passage with your families, friends, or congregation.

Pray that God will set you free of barriers, fill you with fresh hope, expand your vision, quicken his Word, and empower you as an agent of revival. Also spend time praying for a spiritual awakening of your families, churches, community, nation, and beyond.

Re-commission one another to go forth as messengers of hope and agents of revival until you meet again.

Your Choice

In the final analysis, however, overcoming these barriers is also a *choice*. True, hope is a gift from God. But hopefulness is a choice. Your choice. Whether we face sorrows, disappointments, fatigue, or fears, God calls us to choose confidence in him, to choose to hope in him, to choose to fulfill our role as his messengers with boldness and courage.

This was true of Abraham, of whom the Scriptures say, "Against all hope, Abraham in hope believed and so became the father of many nations. . . . Without weakening in his faith, he faced the fact that his body was as good as dead. . . . Yet he did not waiver through unbelief regarding the promise of God, but was strengthened in his faith and gave glory to God, being fully persuaded that God had power to do what he had promised" (Rom. 4:18–21).

It was the choice Micah made within a spiritually bankrupt generation: "But as for me, I watch in hope for the LORD, I wait for God my Savior; my God will hear me. . . . Though I have fallen, I will rise. . . . I will bear the LORD's wrath, until he pleads my case and establishes my right. He will bring me out into the light; I will see his righteousness. . . . The day for building your walls will come, the day for extending your boundaries" (Micah 7:7–11).

Delivering messages called "lamentations," filled with sorrow over God's ensuing judgments upon Jerusalem, Jeremiah chose the way of hope as he proclaimed, "So I say, 'My splendor is gone and all that I had hoped from the LORD.' . . . Yet this I call to mind and therefore I have hope: Because of the LORD's great love we are not consumed, for his compassions never fail. They are new every morning; great is your faithfulness. I say to myself, 'The LORD is my portion; therefore I will wait for him.' The LORD is good to those whose hope is in him" (Lam. 3:18, 21–25). Ultimately Jeremiah persisted as a messenger full of confidence in God because he chose to hope even when his soul felt there was no hope.

Will you also choose to factor in supernatural intervention for those to whom you minister? Only then can you speak and dream as you should. Only then can you break through the barriers of unbelief and become strong as a Messenger of Hope.

As Paul declares in 2 Corinthians 1:18–22, the promises of God are *yes* to us in Christ and guaranteed by the Spirit who seals us. Now we need to speak forth the *Amen!* We must say to God, "I choose to believe you. Let it be done according to your Word. My confidence is in all that you offer in Christ. You are totally dependable. Hope is not in vain. In Christ there is so much more to come for all of us. And I will call others to join with me in the same vision." Then we herald that vision to others.

Our commission as Messengers of Hope is also very much what Joshua gave to the Israelites as they prepared to cross over the Jordan and take possession of the Promised Land: "Consecrate yourselves, for tomorrow the LORD will do amazing things among you" (Josh. 3:5). It is coming, he predicts. Not a long time from now. Tomorrow. What God does for those waiting for him will be utterly amazing. This hope is at hand. Get ready.

The Glad Commission

In a sense, the commission given Isaiah in the fortieth chapter is God's commission to every Messenger of Hope. As opposed to the

Great Commission, I often like to call it the "Glad Commission." Having called us to prepare a way in the wilderness for revealing God's glory before all flesh, having summoned messengers to bring this good news to all of Israel, God then calls them to speak with fearless confidence: "Lift up your voice with a shout, lift it up, do not be afraid; say to the towns of Judah, 'Here is your God!'" (Isa. 40:9). That's the commission. That's the choice before all agents of revival—to speak the vision without fear, to lift up our voices, to even do it with a bold shout. Then we watch God fulfill his promise as he manifests his presence in power among us.

At the age of seventy-seven, he had pastored forty-two years at the fourteen-thousand-member Concord Baptist Church of Christ in Brooklyn's rugged Bedford-Stuyvesant neighborhood. Gardner C. Taylor, an African-American minister called the "prince of preachers," shared in an interview how he was able to sustain his courageous role as a messenger of hope for so long in such a challenging city. Bottom line: He chose to hope, and God took it from there. Says he, "Every time I have felt at the end of my tether, the old promise has come true. There has been restoration; there has been renewal; there has been revival. . . . Sometimes I feel discouraged and think my work's in vain, but *then*, just at the end of my tether; but *then*, when all of my strength seems spent and gone; *then*, when I come almost to the borders of despair; *then*, when I feel frustrated and confused; *then* . . . the Holy Spirit comes and revives my soul again."[14]

Are you fully expecting God to do the same for you as you spread the message of hope? A thousand other agents of revival join Dr. Taylor to testify that God will not fail to empower you, even when your own confidence level is burning low. Whoever you are, in God's hands, *you* can become an agent of revival. It's his call. It's your choice. It's his power.

With such confidence in hand, we now turn in the second half of this book to explore practical considerations on how to deliver the message of hope.

Part Two

The Message

This the House of Prayer for all people, and Lord Jesus, there are moments in our lives when we want to steal away. We want to get away from the clatter of our world and we want to find a quiet place where we can talk face to face with Thee. . . .

Have mercy on us, Lord. We're stealing away because the Black community seems to be under siege again—dope running rampant in our community; hoodlums and thugs have frightened our women; our churches are being broken into; houses are being burglarized; and we seem, our Father, to be destined to destroy ourselves. We need Thee, Jesus. Have mercy on us. . . . Is there a Balm in Gilead? Is there a word from the Lord for those at the bottom of the ladder? Is there a word? Is there a healing word, a word of hope? . . .

Anoint Thy servant this morning, Lord, in the midst of agony, to speak a word to Thy people. The sheep look up in hope, O Lord, that the undershepherd would hear from the Chief Shepherd and will have a word for the children of color, the children of oppression, the disinherited and dispossessed. . . . Let this moment not be in vain. . . . In Your blessed Name and for Your sake we pray this morning. Amen and Amen.

Fred C. Lofton,
"We Need Thee, Lord Jesus, As Never Before" (1993),
taken from *Conversations with God:
Two Centuries of Prayers by African-Americans*

CHAPTER FIVE

H.O.P.E.–Key Ingredients in Every Message of Hope

The church I attend was founded in the 1730s. Like many churches in the Northeast, it is surrounded by a 250-year-old graveyard, including tombstones of Revolutionary War soldiers. At the very front, along the sidewalk leading to the double doors, one tombstone marks the burial place of the church's third pastor. He preached during the First Great Awakening, in the mid 1700s. Passing his tombstone on Sunday morning, I'm reminded how churches all over the world exist, more often than not, as a legacy of some messenger of hope—a pastor, missionary, lay leader—around whom revival converged.

You Are the Message

As we've seen, anyone can be a Messenger of Hope. Our first image may be of a pastor and his preaching. And in a sense, clergy are preeminently such messengers. But as we're about to discover, effective ways of delivering the message of hope are equally applicable to a father or a mother facilitating family devotions at the dinner table, to someone leading an early-morning Bible study on the

Gospels, or to a layperson guiding a city-wide concert of prayer, or to a team leader studying the doctrine of the Holy Spirit with fellow missionaries during a field retreat in India. Of course, it also applies to a pastor preaching on Sunday morning.

In all of these scenarios, the delivery of the message of hope begins inside the messenger himself. To be an effective messenger, you must incarnate the message. What you deliver to others must come out of what is already inside of you. If you are struggling to find an unwavering confidence about coming revival, remember: You are as likely to believe what you preach as you are to preach what you believe. In other words, the more you choose to share the message— even in the face of your own struggles—the more the message will become a part of you and resonate within you. That can't help but make you an even more effective messenger to others.

Delivering the Message

So what does it take to deliver the message effectively? For pastors who ask, many voices claim to have the answer. A well-known school of Christian communications advertises: "Now you can improve your preaching in just five days!" An international congress on preaching in London promises that "a thousand of the world's top preachers" will be in attendance and then asks the question, "Shouldn't you be among them?" To be sure, the average preacher confronts a library of suggestions for being a more effective communicator. Scores of titles have recently been published.

Whatever suggestions are applied, the pastor (or any of us who act as messengers of hope) will not be satisfied that adequate delivery has been made until (in the words of Annie Dillard) the message helps Christians to quit being "cheerful, brainless tourists on a package tour of the Absolute." A pastor's message on a Sunday morning, for example, should transform the hearers into believers who are "wearing crash helmets. Ushers should issue life preservers and signal flares; they should lash us to our pews."[1] I want to give you ideas for doing this that you may not find anywhere else.

Getting Them to Listen

Of course, the first question to ask about our hearers is simple: Are any of them listening? Experts tell us that contemporary Bible teaching needs to be tighter, shorter, crisper, and more relevant. The glut of information coming at the TV generation is at such a rapid rate of transmission that *pacing* in Bible teaching is everything. Pastors are warned that sermons need to have new patterns because many in our audiences are "mosaic thinkers," putting ideas together in new configurations. These people resonate much more with visionary preaching but are also eager for a dialogical approach in which they can participate in the process of arriving at the truths together.[2]

The Four Ingredients

In a recent interview with Bob Buford, head of Texas-based Buford Television Incorporated, the question was asked: "How can preachers [or any messenger for Christ] connect with business leaders in their message?" Buford's answer was quite telling, useful for any agent of revival! He outlined four stages:

The first stage is *connection*. You help the listener to connect with you, as the messenger, and with the real-life situations that are the context for your message.

The second stage is *Scripture*. Now you connect biblical truth with the personal context within which you have set the hearer.

The third stage is *application*. Businesspeople live in an action-oriented world. They want specific action steps spelled out for them. What can they do right now?

The fourth stage is *vehicle*. You should be even more specific, spelling out a practical step that the listener can take as soon as the message is finished.[3]

What struck me as I read the interview was how closely Buford's analysis parallels the four key ingredients for delivering a message of hope. Buford called them connection, Scripture, application, and vehicle. I call them H.O.P.E.:

- Hop on
- Open up
- Pray back
- Enter in

They represent how I have delivered the vision for nearly twenty years.

To spell it out more specifically, an effective Messenger of Hope helps the listeners:

Hop on—by getting them "up to speed" on what God has done before in revival, as well as what he is doing in revival today.

Open up—by teaching them from the Scriptures the promises and ways of God in revivals and explaining why we have every reason to hope for a similar work in our generation.

Pray back—by helping them to pray the message of revival back to God right away, asking him to bring it about just as he promised in his Word.

Enter in—by motivating and equipping them to take one or two practical steps toward preparing for and becoming involved in the coming revival for which we hope and pray.

It is my thesis that these four ingredients need to be a part of every message of hope. Although it's not necessary, there is some logic in following the very order suggested by the acronym H.O.P.E.

As an example, imagine a father is leading his family in evening devotions. He has just ten minutes. He begins by recounting for a minute or two a story he just got off the Internet through the Web site called "Religion News Today." He recounts how a group of pastors in Spokane, Washington, just finished spending forty days in prayer and total fasting. He describes what this must have been like and then reports that a whole new surge of evangelism out of their churches has resulted. *(Hop on.)* Next, he has one of his older children read the short account in 2 Chronicles 15 of what God did through Asa and the revival movement he instigated for Jerusalem. *(Open up.)* Third, he invites his wife and ten-year-old daughter to each pray a short sentence prayer, inviting God to work in their hearts and in their church with new empowerment in ministry, so that they may see others come to Christ as well. *(Pray back.)* Finally, all five in the circle agree to look for one opportunity to speak of Christ to a non-Christian friend within the next twenty-four hours. They'll make this effort as a preliminary step toward what they hope God will do in greater measure with them when he gives the kind of revival they have asked him for tonight. They agree to share the results at tomorrow's dinner. *(Enter in.)*

For the second scenario, travel to a Sunday morning worship service. The pastor has forty minutes in which to preach. Taking H.O.P.E. as his guide, he arbitrarily divides his time into four ten-minute segments. They might run something like this:

Hop on—He shares reports on what God is doing locally, nationally, and internationally to incite Christ's church toward revival. (Later in this book you'll find a number of resources for such information.) His final story tells about the faithfulness of Bible teachers in the revival in China. This prepares his audience for the text.

Open up—Next he preaches expositionally from his text, 2 Corinthians 1:8–11. He tells about a God who raises the dead, even in the most hopeless situations, pressing home the point that what God did for Paul he is doing throughout the church right now in early phases of revival. God is willing to do this in our own congregation, he reassures.

Pray back—Now, for another ten minutes he encourages the congregation to pray back through the passage, verse by verse, in small groups of six, formed all through the sanctuary. Suggesting points for prayer all along the way, he gives them about two minutes apiece on each one. He shapes the final minute with a responsive prayer printed in the bulletin.

Enter in—Finally, the pastor challenges them to spend the coming week watching for evidence of God at work, showing resurrection power in the midst of seeming impossibilities. This may be manifested in their own lives or in reports they hear from other places. In addition, they are challenged to bring one account with them the next week, in order to share briefly with others either in Sunday school or at the beginning of worship.

To help make all of this more specific, at the end of this chapter is a worksheet entitled "Developing Your Own Message of Hope." You may want to study it briefly before going on to the next chapter. Also, plan to refer back to it as you work on your own message of hope, drawing on suggestions and resources in the final four chapters of this book.

My conviction is that the four ingredients—H.O.P. E.—need to be a part of your message of hope everywhere you share it, with every kind of group, and all the time. That's what makes it a real *life*-message.

Immediate Results

As you do share the message of hope, expect immediate results. *Immediate? Is that possible?* Consider:

H—God cannot lead us on the basis of facts we do not have! The more facts you give to get people "up to speed," the more God has to work with to transform listeners into prisoners of hope and to lead them into the promise of revival.

O—The Scriptures are clear; faith comes by hearing God's Word (Rom. 10:17). The more we share this fresh perspective on the Scriptures, unfolding the scope and breadth of hope that permeates his Word, the easier will be the Holy Spirit's job to ignite victorious faith in prisoners of hope. God's Word never returns unproductive (compare Isa. 55:10–11 and Luke 8:11–15).

P—We serve a prayer-answering God, especially when we pray his very Word back to him (1 John 5:14–15). Praying over a message of hope gets believers to raise up prayers they have never uttered before. Such praying transforms the pray-ers; it also transforms the world for which we pray. The results begin immediately in the hearts of hearers who pray sincerely and multiply as God answers prayers for revival in days to come.

E—The more prepared and open God's people are to receive a greater work of God in revival, the more quickly God can move to answer their prayers. In fact, steps of preparation for revival are, in many ways, the very first phase of the revival for which we hope.

I do not share these four ingredients as a foolproof formula. Nor is H.O.P.E. simply a gimmick. This approach is how I've delivered the message of hope for many years to audiences around the world, whether few or large in number. It has taken shape for me over time, and has worked in real-life challenges.

One thing I can tell you with certainty: These four ingredients are so incredibly potent because I have always insisted that my central message is not ultimately a message of revival. Rather, I have tried to focus my message preeminently on the person of Christ. He is what the coming revival is all about. He is its source and its goal. Our effectiveness to herald a comprehensive vision of Christ is what allows us to succeed as agents of revival. It happens too infrequently in too many churches. But this is the most important, the most practical of all principles for delivering our message.

Developing Your Own Message of Hope

Note: Useful in preparing family devotions, small group Bible studies, or a Sunday morning sermon, this thirty-minute approach represents only one way to deliver the message of hope. No one message, however, can incorporate all of these suggestions.

1. If you were to give your Bible study, family devotions, or Sunday morning message a title, what would it be? What is the theme for this session? What facet of the vision for revival do you want to explore?

   What principle(s) of God's work in personal or corporate revival do you want to illustrate in this session? How might you do that?

2. What text have you selected? (Everything should be built around the Scriptures somehow. In a sense, the entire thirty minutes should reinforce the Word of God.)

3. Do you want to begin with an opening statement? Observation? Story? If so, what should it be?

4. *Hop on!* (four to five minutes)

   Do you have a story that will alert your listeners to God's ways in revivals in the past? What story could you share from church history?

   Do you have a story that will alert listeners to what God is doing in revival today? Locally? Nationally? Or somewhere else in the world?

   Is there a story that will help your people sense the hope they can have personally for a greater work of God in their own lives?

   Do you want to share an illustration from your own life or from the life of someone else in the congregation that will enlarge understanding of what God can/will do in true revival?

Above all: What are some exciting ways to strengthen your listeners' confidence in God—that he is the God of all hope, that he is at work to advance the kingdom of his dear Son, and that he will not fail to pour out increased blessings upon them, individually and corporately? How can you open your message by calling them again to a renewed hope in God for their own lives, as well as for our generation?

5. *Open up!* (twelve minutes)

Read the text (two minutes)

Share (or preach) from the text. (See questions in chapter 8.)

How will you show your listeners from the text that God is the God of "so much more," the God of hope?

How will you relate this text to the overall themes of revival and spiritual awakening?

How will you make Christ the central issue throughout your study of the text? (See questions in chapter 6.)

6. *Pray back!* (ten minutes)

Will you pray verse by verse? Through the message outline? By some other approach?

What creative format could you use? Pairs? Triplets? Small groups? Responsive prayers? Sentence prayers? Unison prayers? Prayers by leaders from the front? Times of silence? Be open, creative, and biblical.

7. *Enter in!* (three minutes)

Conclude by recommending one specific step listeners could take next to help them "act as if" God will answer their prayers. First, how could this message help them pray differently during the week? Also what should they do, based on the text and the message, to get ready—or to be better prepared—for renewal and revival as God gives it?

Do you want to end with a closing statement? Appeal? Brief anecdote? Brief prayer?

Oh thou God of all nations upon the earth! we thank thee, that thou art *no respecter of persons,* and that thou *hast made of one blood all nations of men.* . . . We thank thee, that the sun of righteousness has at last shed morning beams upon them. *Rend thy heavens,* O Lord, and *come down* upon the earth; and grant that *the mountains,* which now obstruct the perfect day of thy goodness and mercy towards them, may *flow down at thy presence.* Send thy gospel, we beseech thee, among them. May the nations, which now *sit in darkness,* behold and rejoice in its *light.* May *Ethiopia soon stretch out her hands unto thee,* and lay hold of the gracious promise of thy everlasting covenant. . . . O, hasten that glorious time, when the knowledge of the gospel of Jesus Christ, shall cover the *earth, as the waters cover the sea.*

Absalom Jones,
"A Thanksgiving Prayer for the Abolition
of the African Slave Trade" (1808),
taken from *Conversations with God:
Two Centuries of Prayers by African-Americans*

CHAPTER SIX

CHRIST: THE HEART OF THE MESSAGE OF HOPE

B ill Gates of Microsoft, claimed by many to be "man of the century," is referenced 25,000 times on the World Wide Web. Jesus Christ, on the other hand, appears 146,000 times. But he's the only topic of conversation in heaven! Frankly, Christ is the "man of the ages," the one who therefore must dominate every message of hope, day by day.

Our only hope as a nation is to flood the church—and even more importantly, the movement of prayer ascending in the church—with heralds of the hope of revival. These heralds must be, heart and soul, singularly messengers of Christ—the *whole* Christ.

Consumed with Christ

In C. S. Lewis's *The Silver Chair,* one of the *Chronicles of Narnia,* a dreadfully thirsty little girl named Jill finds herself tempted by a stream of water that is guarded by a fearsome looking lion named Aslan (the Christ figure in the Narnia series). So overcome by thirst, "she almost felt she would not mind being eaten by the lion if only she could be sure of getting a mouthful of water first." Jill asks and receives permission to come and drink. The lion's voice frightens her so much, however, that she is not sure she wants to risk advancing to the stream.

> "Will you promise not to—do anything to me, if I do come?"
> "I make no promise," said the Lion. . . .
> "Do you eat girls?" she said.
> "I have swallowed up girls and boys, women and men, kings and emperors, cities and realms," said the Lion. . . .
> "I daren't come and drink," said Jill.
> "Then you will die of thirst," said the Lion. "There is no other stream."
> It was the worst thing she had ever had to do, but she went forward. . . .[1]

Here's the tension every Christian should feel within when we hear prospects of revival proclaimed, if proclaimed properly. Around Christ flows a river of blessing sufficient to quench our deepest thirst, as well as the longings of a whole generation. We are invited to drink with abandon. But he will consume us in the process! Or rather, we will be consumed with him. Is this the vision of Christ offered in your message of hope? It should be.

From her years of ministering to the poorest of the poor in Calcutta, Mother Teresa cautions, "If the words we speak do not bring the light of Christ, they only serve to make the darkness worse."[2] That's true anywhere. If our message is not a message of Christ and his all-consuming life, then it will leave people with less hope and more despair than if we had never come.

Obviously, therefore, the *content* of our message is a very serious matter. There's nothing more practical we can do to ensure its proper delivery than to determine that Christ will always be the heart of all we share. "When Jesus Christ fascinates—and the Interpreter Spirit specializes in making Jesus fascinating—we will be constantly seeking to find and we will be constantly finding, imaginative ways to proclaim him—and him only—to our time."[3]

Christ Is Our Hope

Return to Zechariah 9. What God announced to prisoners of waterless pits that transforms them into prisoners of hope is the message of Christ's triumphal entry (vv. 8–11)—not only into Jerusalem, but among the nations and into the hearts of his people (9:13–10:12). It is a message of massive revival centered on Jesus. That's the decree! He, and he alone, is their assurance that God will restore to them "twice as much" (9:12).

What, after all, is life without hope? And what is hope, in the end, without Christ? All of God's promises are "Yes!" to us in Jesus (2 Cor. 1:20). By his resurrection we've been born again to a living hope (1 Peter 1:3). Every prophetic vision ever given entails greater revelations of who Jesus is (Rev. 19:10). Therefore, the more comprehensive our message of Christ, the more convincing the hope we offer our hearers, and the more compelling our call will be for them to pray and prepare for revival.

Hope reigns because Christ reigns. Hope is a person (1 Tim. 1:1) who comes into the midst of his church to guarantee and lead us into the fulfillment of every glorious prospect God has ordained (Col. 1:27). God offers no hope beyond who Christ is. The eternal past has known no other future but Jesus, and the eternal future knows no other past except him. Of course he's the heart of our message of hope! How could it be otherwise?

In a sense, the whole Reformation was about this truth, about lifting people out of a despairing vision of themselves into the most magnificent vision possible of who Christ is.[4] Recall the stunning christological texts of Ephesians 1, Colossians 1, or Hebrews 1: Can you imagine taking these texts and substituting any other name in heaven or on earth for the name of Jesus?[5] Our doctrine of revival must paint a vision that is preeminently about Christ himself. What more can we ever do for our hearers if we don't do this? We've done them no favor if we rally them to seek a God-given spiritual awakening but with a limited vision of a diminished Christ. The absurdity of such an effort needs no comment. If it is a full revival we want, then a full Christ must be its declared hope.

In Hebrews, for example, Paul calls a persecuted church to press on in courage and hope (3:6) because their eyes are fixed on the Christ ahead of us (12:1–2), the center of the universe (1:1–3), who is the "better hope" (7:19) for all the ages to come (12:22–29). "Let us hold unswervingly to the hope we profess," Hebrews charges us (10:23), because he is coming, bringing the consummation with him (10:25, 37–39). In the power of the Spirit, the future has already begun (6:4–5). God simply wants to pour out more and more of it through Jesus (4:14–16; 13:20–21).

In *The Majestic Tapestry,* church historian Robert E. Webber speaks of his own "conversion" to this higher view of Christ and the need to keep such a vision central in all ministry. He writes:

> My view of the work of Christ was severely limited. It wasn't that I didn't believe the right truth. I simply didn't understand how far-reaching and all-inclusive the work of Christ really was. When I discovered the universal and cosmic nature of the work of Christ, it was like being born again. I was given a key to a Christian way of viewing the whole world, a key that unlocked the door to a rich storehouse of spiritual treasures, treasures that I am still handling in sheer amazement.[6]

While researching his book *The Jesus I Never Knew,* Philip Yancey entered into the same personal awakening. He reached the conclusion that he was a Christian for two basic reasons—because he lacked any good alternatives and because of who Jesus is. Drawing from Martin Luther, he likens Christ to the focal point of a fine painting being examined by a magnifying glass. The object in the center of the glass stays crisp and clear, while around the edges the view grows increasingly distorted. "For me, Jesus has become the focal point. I learned in the process of writing this book to keep the magnifying glass of my faith focused on Jesus."[7] Jesus is also the focal point—the magnifying glass—for every agent of revival, for every message of hope. In the end, either we preach Christ in all of his magnificence—how in him the sovereign initiatives of grace envelop our lives—or we end up delivering a message that's mainly about human potential and abilities, "with Christ brought in only to boost us and help us achieve that potential."[8]

Heralds of revival are actually ambassadors of the cross, because the only hope we offer is defined by Calvary—the utter necessity of divine intervention as the only hope for our human, sinful state. Revival is simply another manifestation of the message of the cross. The Reformation argued the difference between a "theology of glory," where we attempt higher spirituality by our efforts toward God, and a "theology of the cross," in which we confess ourselves to be constantly bankrupt, always desperate for God's initiative in Christ. If we are to know the glory of Christ, he must infuse us with fuller revelations of himself. That's why revival—a spiritual awakening—is the single greatest blessing the church can anticipate between the cross and the second coming.

Quite naturally, Christ occupies the heart, the center, the focal point of every revival. Because he makes it possible. Because he's what it's all about. Therefore, if we lack interest in revival, it may really mean, in the end, that we lack vision for (or understanding of) the centrality of Christ and his cross in all the ways of God.

Three Dimensions of the Message of Hope

In *The Hope at Hand*, I discussed three dimensions of a Christ-centered revival, which correspond to the three dimensions of every message of hope. The words I use to describe the impact of revival are *focus, fullness, fulfillment*. Here's what I wrote:

> (1) In revival there is a *new focus* on Christ's person (who he is *to* us, especially his character as God's Son) and on his passion (who he is *for* us, especially in his death, resurrection, and ascension). As a result, (2) we experience together in new ways *the fullness of his life* over us (as he rules *over* us as Lord and Head of the church) and in us (as he *indwells* us with resurrection power). (3) All of this presses us into new involvements in the *fulfillment of Christ's mission* where we live, and among the nations, as he carries out his purposes (*through* us), and as he establishes his preeminence among many peoples (going *out ahead of us* to lead his global cause to victory and to bring about the consummation of all things).[9]

Focus, fullness, fulfillment—no outline could be more practical for helping you design any message of hope from the Scriptures. To use a technical theological term, these words "exegete" biblical renewal.

In fact, if you study texts of the great "revival prayers" of the Scriptures—including Jesus' extended prayer in John 17 (and even what's known as the Lord's Prayer)—you will find that these three concepts are the consistent heart-cry every time. "Show us your glory!" Focus. Only Christ embodies all that glory. "Fill us with your power and presence!" Fullness. As that happens, we are seen to be nothing less than the body (community) of Christ. "Release us to advance your kingdom victoriously!" Fulfillment. Christ is the one we serve, promote, proclaim. Our mission goes forward as it amplifies his ministry through us, and vindicates it afresh "with a demonstration of the Spirit's power" (1 Cor. 2:4).

That's how the church prayed in Acts 4, and that's how it preached in the ensuing chapters. Whole cities were captivated by their vision of Christ as a result. How can Christians today labor for less?

Message or Mascot?

Unfortunately, the way Christ is heard or seen in many of our churches falls short of this. For many of our people, he is very much (using Stephen Carter's term) a "hobby," not much different from building model airplanes or bowling.[10] In many of our churches, the Christ we preach may actually trivialize God, making him into "a deity who fits nicely within precise doctrinal positions, who lends almighty support to social crusades, or who conforms to individual spiritual experiences." We have "pared God down to more manageable proportions."[11]

Our domestication of Christ, coupled with our privatization of the gospel, renders him no bigger to us than personal dreams, daily relationships, inner emotional needs, or church agendas—in other words, our ongoing struggles for survival. Many have chosen to come to Christ, but only as far as we have to come in order to get our needs met. "If you listen to much of our preaching, you get the impression that Jesus was some sort of itinerant therapist who, for free, traveled about helping people feel better."[12]

I ask you: Who is the Jesus being proclaimed in our land? In your church? To your family? How much of our message about him—and, as a result, any discussion of spiritual awakening to him—rises essentially out of market-driven ministries that make the "customers" the controlling factor in what message we peddle? How often has Christ simply formed our product, packaged for maximum sales? Says missionary theologian Leslie Newbigin, "I suddenly saw that . . . someone could use all the language of evangelical Christianity, and yet the center was fundamentally the Self, my need of salvation. And God is auxiliary to that."[13]

In other words, as I often say, Christ is more or less evangelicalism's *mascot*. Let me illustrate. I attended a high school that was football crazy, with a stadium seating twenty thousand. The school produced nearly twenty-five state championship teams, and our teams were voted national champions more than once. Called the Massillon Tigers, our mascot was a student dressed up as a tiger—wearing real tiger skin, in fact. At times in the midst of a game—if we were falling behind or if the crowd needed to be stirred to cheer the team on to victory or when it served the coach's purpose—the uniformed mascot would run his stripes onto the field. Seeing the tiger doubled our determination to put bold plays into action, to fight and struggle, to win the game on our terms. Time-out was called. The mascot appeared. The crowd cheered. The team regained courage and resolve. Then the mascot disappeared to the sidelines to await another crisis. Immediately everyone felt better, and the game proceeded.

While visiting churches on some Sunday mornings, I've felt that Jesus is also being deployed as our mascot. Once a week we trot him out (so to speak), to cheer us up, to give us new vigor and vision, to reinforce for us the great things we might do for God, or to reignite a celebration of the victory we know we will win. For the rest of the week, however, he's pretty much relegated to the sidelines. Even during Sunday school, worship, or sermons, I've noted how references to him serve mostly to buttress teachings on "How to Have a Healthy Family," or "Godly Ways to Handle Your Finances," or "Our Responsibilities in World Evangelism." Our songs may mention him (or may not), but great hymns or choruses designed to unfold the scope of his character, his reign, and the abounding hope he brings are few and far between.

In a sense, we've been diverted from him with inordinate affections. We prize ambitions of the evangelical enterprise more than we embrace Christ as our Prize. "The erosion of a Christ-centered faith threatens to undermine the identity of evangelical Christianity . . . real revival and genuine reformation will not be built on flimsy foundations."[14]

This awful deficiency threatens all who wish to become Messengers of Hope. We must labor more than we might guess to keep Christ as the heart of our message and to be sure our hearers know that's what we're doing. We must be the magnifying glasses of which Luther and Yancey spoke. The H.O.P.E. approach to giving a message of hope, to be explored more deeply in the next four chapters, is of virtually no significance, no matter how effectively we may employ these devices, unless . . . unless when we're finished, people are looking only at Christ, beholding him as the summation of the revival we seek.

We're on a Campaign

In Acts 1:8, Jesus sent out witnesses, not just *for* him but *unto* him. Bottom-line service to God for all believers is the preaching of his Son (Rom. 1:9). Every Messenger of Hope should say that "when God, who set me apart from birth and called me by his grace, was pleased to reveal his Son in me, so that I might preach him among the Gentiles, I did not consult any man" (Gal. 1:15–16). To speak out "the unsearchable riches of Christ," and to make crystal clear to everyone "the administration of this mystery" (Eph. 3:8–9)—what a privilege! Only through "the proclamation of Jesus Christ, according to the revelation of the mystery" (Rom. 16:25), will our hearers be established by God in their understanding of every hope before us. Our job is to multiply prisoners of hope as we "take captive every thought to make it obedient to Christ" (2 Cor. 10:5).

As suggested earlier, it's somewhat like campaigning for a presidential candidate. We want to highlight our leader's strengths and accomplishments, fill people with hope about what he is able to accomplish, articulate the compelling promises that make up his platform, help people envision what it would be like for him to be completely in charge, and incite them to appropriate action (which means focusing daily discipleship on him and the prospects of revival in him). Messengers of Hope campaign for Christ, declaring that he who is Lord indeed is ready to awaken us to his presence *in deed,* in the midst of our need.

Christ and Consummation

Over the years a helpful word for me, in defining the comprehensive dimensions of proclaiming Christ as our hope, has been *consummation.* My next book, *Christ and Consummation,* will focus exclusively on this. For now, let me summarize what I've discovered.

The word *consummation* means to complete something in every detail, to give the ultimate manifestation, to bring about the climax or grand finale, to be fully engaged in something, to consume or be consumed by something totally. Biblically, this is what Christ is always prepared to do. As C. S. Lewis's Aslan makes clear, he is determined to be all-consuming, and to have us consumed with him. That's where he's headed as he takes us into God's future for our lives, for the nations, and for the whole creation. He is our destination. The climax of all our hopes is lodged in him. He will one day be the center of *the* consummation. Even so, he wants to be the consuming issue in all of our lives right now. Revival powerfully reveals God's commitment to this. So should our message of hope.

Only Christ encompasses and amplifies all of God's promises from Genesis to Revelation. He guarantees their full flowering; he will complete them. In that sense, history is teleological—focused on the end. The sweep of human events—including events in the church and around the church in every generation—are moving us toward the day when Christ's preeminence will be manifested unchallenged throughout the universe. The Christ with whom we are united is, right now, "the presence of the future."[15]

Therefore, every message of hope we share with others must highlight how God's promises are all shaped by the horizon of the consummation itself. Consider these two passages:

> Nevertheless, when everything created has been made subject to God, then shall the Son himself be subject to God, who gave him power over all things. Thus, in the end, shall God be wholly and absolutely God.
>
> 1 Corinthians 15:28 PHILLIPS

> For God has allowed us to know the secret of his plan, and it is this: he purposed long ago in his sovereign will that all human history should be consummated in Christ, that everything that exists in Heaven or earth shall find its perfection and fulfillment in him.
>
> Ephesians 1:10 PHILLIPS

Here's my question: Can we ever herald the true Christ to our own generation if our message falls short of this vision? Does he want to give us less than abundant approximations of this vision in our own day? After all, the Spirit regularly takes the glories of Christ ascended and reveals them to us, showing us things to come (John 16:13–15). Can we do less whenever we speak of Christ? With him there is always so much more. The Holy Spirit brings dramatically near to us a wide hope, because it's embodied entirely in Christ. He's the air we breathe. Though perhaps not yet chronologically near, all hope is *christologically* near, as near as the Jesus who indwells his church right now.

Think of the consummation as God's "final revival." It's the greatest renewal imaginable—a renovated heaven and earth (2 Peter 3:10–14), covered with a knowledge of Christ like waters cover the sea (Hab. 2:14). From the final revival, therefore, all other revivals must take their cue. In principle, no prophecy exists in Scripture about the consummation that is not capable of being realized (at least in some measure) within history. Just look at the explosion of wonders and miracles all through the Book of Acts. Of course, the perfect manifestation of revival requires the ultimate intervention of God, which we call the second coming of Christ. However, anytime when God invades his church with a surprisingly refreshing outpouring of the Spirit, he brings to us "approximations of the consummation" (my personal phrase for revival, discussed in *The Hope at Hand*). We taste of the final revival, when the Lamb will shine on us forever from the midst of the throne (Rev. 21:22–24; 22:3–4).

William Carey, a father of modern missions, understood this when he published his research on the unevangelized in 1792. Having prayed nearly seven years for revival in a concert of prayer in Northampton, England, he confronted his denomination's annual meeting as a Messenger of Hope. Drawing from texts in Isaiah on revival—most of them related to the final revival—he wrote and spoke a most arresting vision. Armed with missiological statistics, he first argued for a christology big enough to take to the nations, as well as to mobilize the church to action. In the end, his message created a hope that broke the missionary log-jam on both sides of the Atlantic.

My point in all of this? We have a God who wants to do so much more for us, both now (approximations) and in the final revival (consummation). How? Through the Person at the center of the final revival and of every other revival. That's why the Spirit's mission to us is to accelerate, intensify, deepen, expand, extend, and increasingly fill out for every generation of believers all that Jesus is meant to be for us. He longs to renew us today with substantial installments of that supreme epoch when all our hopes will reach their climax.

Peter teaches that Christ, when properly proclaimed, becomes a "morning star" (2 Peter 1:19), alerting us that dawn is about to break upon us from God (see also Rev. 22:16). As a Messenger of Hope, the most practical suggestion I can make is this: Every time you deliver the hope, be sure that Jesus is more than ever a Morning Star for those who hear you. If you do this, then you will truly become an agent of revival.

Practical Questions to Help You

As you set to work teaching the Scriptures (in whatever capacity), consider the following set of questions. They can help you unlock any passage on hope, making it a more Christ-centered message for those to whom God sends you. For each text, ask the following:

What specific facets or dimensions of hope does this passage set before us? Base your study on the three key dimensions of revival: Does it promise a sharper God-given *focus* on the person of Christ? Does it offer a deeper experience of the *fullness* of Christ in our life together? Does it point toward a greater *fulfillment* of the mission of Christ where we live and beyond?

In what sense is Christ himself the summation of the hope described in these verses?

How will this hope, centered on Christ, be ultimately expressed in the consummation? What will it look like then? How does this help me better understand the hope—especially for my generation?

Why must Jesus be the center of the hope at any point of its expression, but especially when it reaches its climax? Why is he so critical to the outworking of this hope?

To what degree is God willing, able, and ready to give us right now approximations of all this hope promises? How might this hope find new manifestations in our lives right now? What would this look like?

If God were to unleash a fresh work of revival in our church or throughout the whole body of Christ in a way that provided significant experiences of the hope offered in this passage, what might happen? What would be the impact on individuals? On families? On churches? On a whole nation? In what sense might this revival be called a general awakening to Christ?

Specifically, based on this text, how should we begin to pray and prepare for a work of revival right now?

Dis-illusion Them

As Oswald Chambers remarked in *My Utmost for His Highest,* the church needs to come under "the discipline of dis-illusionment."[16] Christ is the touchstone for all reality. "These [religious rituals] are a shadow of the things that were to come; the reality, however, is found in Christ" (Col. 2:17). We need to study him and him preeminently, until we discard all illusions arising out of discipleship not centered on him for who he *really* is. When our hearers are similarly dis-illusioned, they are ready to embrace the hope of revival, the hope of shadows turned to reality. That's our job. To dis-illusion them. That's one incomparable blessing brought to others by every true agent of revival.

Survey the issues raised in this chapter. Ponder the challenge of helping the church rethink who is at the center of its message of hope. Then reflect on two final questions: How would you describe the emphasis Christ receives in the messages *you* bring to God's people by preaching, by teaching, by counseling, by parenting, and by your very life? Second, would you like to make any changes in the emphasis of your messages in order to make Christ more the heart of the hope you share? If so, how would you do this?

We enjoy saying the Lord gives us the living bread.

Look to God, be faithful to God, and say no more. . . . God comes in you to do. Humble yourselves that Christ may be your portion.

Speaking from a sign of God, a cleaver. The day of the Lord never comes till the signs of the Lord appear. Man in God's hand is a sign. Thou art my battle axe, my weapon of war. God's wonders coming, doing a strange work. Ministers of God preaching the word out of season and in season.

God standing a wonder in man. Who can hinder God; His wonders are telling. We delight to see Jesus in signs. Confirming us out from snares, Jesus, great God at hand. His word telling about his ways bring us out from the mystery of evil. Watching for his wonders; telling God, I believe.

Charles Harrison Mason,
"An Exhortative Invocation" (1919),
taken from *Conversations with God:
Two Centuries of Prayers by African-Americans*

CHAPTER SEVEN

H Stands for "Hop On!"

***Hop* On!**
Open Up!
Pray Back!
Enter In!

I live in metro New York, home of a most famous (or infamous!) subway system. Laid out on many levels and moving in many different directions, it can overwhelm the uninitiated visitor. But get a subway map and suddenly you find courage to finally hop on a train and go somewhere. In the same way, God's people need a map of revival so that they can have the courage to pray and prepare for what is coming.

The first ingredient of every message of hope is "Hop on!" This phrase reminds us that agents of revival help God's people get up to speed with how God has worked in past awakenings, as well as how he is bringing forth renewal and revival today—in churches, communities, throughout our nation, and worldwide.

News Makes News

From previous revivals, we know that verbal communication is possibly the most important single *human* factor in the spread of spiritual breakthroughs. "News of awakening tends to stimulate awakening."[1] The more people hear of what God has done in the past or is doing in other places, the bolder they become in faith that God could do the same where they live. As we discovered in chapter 3, this is a wonderful first step toward becoming a prisoner of hope.

Of course, we need to help people develop "interpretative skills" so they quickly grasp what God is really doing. Recently, for example, missionary scholar Robertson McQuilkin, looking across the global landscape, interpreted for others what he saw this way:

> *We are winning!* Two centuries ago there was one Christian to every 49 unsaved persons in the world. Today there is one Bible-believing Christian to every nine in the world. . . . *We are losing!* There are more lost persons now living than the total of all who have lived and died throughout all recorded human history. . . . *Both truths are needed:* the task remaining is vastly greater than it ever was before. But the resources and momentum to do it are greater, too.[2]

Notice the balance, the fresh perspective. McQuilkin presents reasonable arguments for seeking revival. His statistics also help us clarify and receive a realistic picture of what God is actually doing. He helps us "hop on."

Using a Catherine Marshall image, it's like flying south in an airplane while the sun is setting. Those sitting to the east see only a darkened sky. Those sitting by the windows looking west see "a sunset suffusing the entire sky with glorious color." In a sense, everyone on the plane is headed for the same destination; which window we look out will not change that destination. But how much more wonderful it is to help people on the left-hand side of the plane to view the sunset on the right![3] That is the first job of the messenger of hope. "Hop on!" we say. "Lift your eyes to see what God is doing all around the world; then you will say 'Truly, the Lord's great power goes far beyond our borders!'" (Mal. 1:5 TLB). Hear the stories. See the glories. Be filled with great expectations.

"You answer us with awesome deeds of righteousness, O God our Savior, the hope of all the ends of the earth" (Ps. 65:5). And so he does! But how many of our people can recount those awesome deeds? How many of them have good reason to believe Christ alone is truly the hope for all nations? They're waiting to be brought up to

speed. Begin feeding them with hope-filled accounts of personal and corporate transformations, recorded in the great revivals of the church. Tell them, as well, what God is doing today in China, Finland, South Africa, or Brazil.

Every promise fulfilled and every report of fulfillment confirm that similar demonstrations of God's faithfulness await all of us, where we live. God is no respecter of persons. What he has done for others—and what he is doing this hour in his church and among the nations—he is willing to do for all. It may not look identical to his works elsewhere, but *in principle* every promise of God actively bears down on each of our families and churches. Notice how Jesus, proclaiming the hope of God's kingdom, declared it "at hand," impending, sweeping over them. New triumphs of grace, he claimed, were poised to break forth. Believing this truth and sharing it with confidence compels our hearers to want to jump on board.

Fostering a Spirit of Suspense

Twenty years ago, in audience after audience, I watched God move as we used a newly released twenty-minute videotape. Really, it was nothing more than a "talking head" featuring the late Dr. J. Edwin Orr (the foremost historian at the time on spiritual awakenings). As he recounted the impact of the first three Great Awakenings in our nation, viewers encountered stories and dramas they had never heard before. I saw their faith and hope in God freshly ignited. They went home to tell others the happy stories.

Missiologist Ralph Winter recommends that all Christians should have two books beside their bed: One nightstand should cradle a Bible, to be consulted with prayer every morning. The other should hold a good church history book (he recommends Kenneth Scott Latourette's *History of Christianity*) to be consulted with prayer before retiring. His reason? The explosive combination of hope-filled kingdom advances recounted in both Bible history and church history will spoil us for anything less than powerful movements of Christ in our own times. I've found he's absolutely right.

To all this, we must also add stories of God's wonders in our generation. For example, what if you told your hearers (your family, small group, or Sunday morning congregation) how the Hindu kingdom of Nepal has been so saturated with the gospel that in the past thirty years the church has grown from twenty-five known believers to over four hundred thousand in two thousand different churches? What if you quoted the recent words of a church leader there who said, "We have experienced a supernatural visitation. There is just no other explanation." And this despite years of great persecution and suffering!

What if you announced that a West Coast city has experienced an amazing evangelistic surge, streaming from the faith and prayers of fifty or so pastors who spent four days in fasting and prayer for revival. What if you told how the city has been turned upside-down, how the churches have exploded numerically and spiritually, how there's been reconciliation among believers across the body of Christ? What if you quoted one of the pastors who interpreted this outpouring, saying: "This has given *all* of us hope to believe once more that God is able."

What if you reported how one of the world's major cults has recently embraced biblical Christianity—turning from their false doctrines, giving up reputation, funding, and lands, in order to follow Jesus Christ in full allegiance to him as their only Lord and Savior? What if you shared how the president of this former cult gives the Holy Spirit credit for a genuine spiritual awakening among hundreds of thousands of members, leading them to make Christ, and Christ alone, their message?

These are true stories—just a sample of what God is doing all around the world today! And how much people need to hear these accounts. Sitting in their "waterless pits" of discouragement and exhaustion, they need to be rehydrated by the living water of all God is able and willing to do! Introduce them to great revivals of the past—like those under Patrick of Ireland, Bernard of Clairvaux, Francis of Assisi, John Wycliffe of England, Sojourner Truth of America, Pandita Ramabai of India, and Festo Kivengere of East Africa. We want to leave people with a spirit of suspense, wondering, "Is another global great awakening just around the corner?"

Story Sources

Where do you find this kind of information? Where do these stories come from? In addition to *The Hope at Hand,* consider the following sources.

Books

More books on the topic of revival appear practically every month. Here are just a few recent titles:

Robert Bakke, *The Concert of Prayer: Back to the Future?* (Evangelical Free Church Press).

Henry T. Blackaby and Claude V. King, *Fresh Encounters: Experiencing God in Spiritual Awakening and Revival* (Broadman & Holman).

Bill Bright, *The Coming Revival: America's Call to Fast, Pray, and Seek the Face of God* (New Life Press).

Robert Coleman, *The Coming World Revival* (Crossway).

Wesley Duewel, *Revival Fire* (Zondervan).

Keith Hardman, *Seasons of Refreshing: Evangelism and Revivals in America* (Baker).

Martyn Lloyd-Jones, *Revival* (Crossway).

Richard Lovelace, *Dynamics of Spiritual Life* (InterVarsity Press).

David McKenna, *The Coming Great Awakening* (Crossway).

J. Edwin Orr, *The Flaming Tongue, The Eager Feet, The Fervent Prayer, and Campus Aflame* (Moody).

Tom Phillips, *Revival Signs: Join the New Spiritual Awakening* (Vision House).

Periodicals

Key periodicals in your mailbox can provide you with fresh stories in every issue. A representative selection may include publications such as:

Charisma

Christianity Today

Concerts of Prayer International newsletter (Chicago and New York)

Global Harvest newsletter (related to A.D. 2000 movement)

Intercessors for America newsletter (Washington, D.C.)

International Renewal Ministries newsletter (Pastors' Prayer Summit, Portland, Oregon)

Mission Frontiers (U.S. Center for World Missions)

National Network of Youth Ministries newsletter (San Diego)

New Man (Promise Keepers)

Pray! (NavPress/National Prayer Committee)

Prism (Evangelicals for Social Action)

The Reconciler (John Perkins Foundation)

Spirit of Revival (Life Action Ministries)

World

World Pulse (Evangelical Missions Information Service)

World Wide Web

Don't stop there, however! Increasingly, updated revival information is available on the World Wide Web. Check a search engine for current URLs for:

Campus Crusade for Christ

Christianity Today

Concerts of Prayer International

Mission America

Promise Keepers

Religion News Today

U.S. Center for World Mission

The U.S. Prayer Track

Youth with a Mission

Mission America, for example, has established an Internet Web site to assist in this communication process. The site, located at

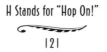
http://www.missionamerica.org, is designed to give browsers more information about how God is at work in America and how they can pray for these exciting undertakings. The site includes key links to other web sites providing additional information on prayer, evangelism, outreach, partnering, and items of interest to the Christian community. Questions may be directed to the Mission America Webmaster at 105240.1005@Compuserve.com.

Local News

Beyond all this, you must also uncover and report accounts of awakening right where you live. Ask other believers regularly in your community this one tantalizing question: What is one way God has manifested more of the presence and power of Christ in your life or in your church this past year, past month, or past week? You might have a number of "reporters" put their findings on an e-mail that can be sent to anyone interested. In a similar vein, local pastors—especially if they are praying together—might set up e-mail connections so they can immediately share the signs of revival they observe in their own churches, as well as throughout the community. Simply tapping into your e-mail once a week could provide you more illustrations than you can unload in all your times of Bible teaching. What a delight it is to watch people get up to speed with what God is doing right around them.

Or, dig even deeper. When you come together for Bible study, as a family, or on Sunday morning, alert everyone that they will have opportunity to share with each other how they have witnessed God's moving toward revival in the past week in their own lives. Or, they might testify to something they discovered in reading accounts of revival somewhere else.

Three Categories of Stories

Are you ready to prepare to help other Christians "hop on"? If so, let me suggest, whatever you do, that over time you help your hearers to discover exciting answers to three questions.

1. *What Is Revival and Why Is It Important?*

Remind people that revival is a divine pattern to be found throughout Scriptures and throughout the history of the church. Give examples.

Tell stories that define clearly and biblically what revival is. Tell them in as uncomplicated a way as possible.

Be creative in how you tell the stories. Make them enticing so that Christians will long for such works of God in their own lives.

Share selections from key books on revival, reading aloud what others say on the topic.

2. *Why Is Revival Needed Today?*

Illustrate how hopeless our national and world situations are if the church is not revived.

Illustrate how paralyzed and helpless the church is to fulfill the work God has given us to do; emphasize that our only hope is to be revived again.

Use illustrations that are both local, national, and global in scope. Show similarities to your own context.

3. *What Are the "Signs of Revival"?*

Tell stories of divine awakenings in other parts of the body of Christ today, so that your hearers might gain hope of what God can do for them.

Give specific emphasis to unique trends in renewal and revival, particularly the movement of prayer (which is always the first phase of any genuine revival).

Tell about exciting advances in local and world evangelization that have come out of preliminary experiences of revival.

Create a sense of expectation in your audience that God is no respecter of persons—that what he is doing with others, he is willing, in principle, to do with you, as well, and even more!

One more effort remains for you, one that is absolutely crucial to get people up to speed and help them "hop on" to what God is up to. You must also testify to your own sense of confidence, showing enthusiasm and conviction as you share these stories of hope.

A. W. Tozer said, "God dwells in a state of perpetual enthusiasm. . . . he pursues his labors always in a fullness of holy zeal. . . . Those first disciples burned with a steady inward fire. They were enthusiastic to the point of complete abandonment."[4] Somehow, in a way that fits your personality, you need to infect people with enthusiasm that will set them on fire. Do you have stories to tell? Are they exciting to you? Then let those you teach feel your zeal.

In the end, all the efforts I've outlined should get *immediate* results. Why? Because God cannot lead you on the basis of facts you do not have. Every time you share these stories, you are placing in the hands of the Holy Spirit more facts with which he can lead your hearers into greater hope and passion for revival—more information than he has ever had to work with before. He will not remain indifferent to these increased opportunities! He will use your stories—and your passion—to incite his people to grab hold, to become prisoners of hope.

With your hearers standing on tiptoe, you now have them ready to dig into the Scriptures.

Scriptures are signs of the only Christ, the glory of God. From the Scriptures Jesus spoke to the minds of the people, and they looked at Him and marveled. Jesus showing forth the wisdom of God. Jesus the sign spoken against. Jesus, a sign overturning the evil time; gathers the nation with His understanding and binds His children together as one. Jesus, the wonder among nations, having done the work He came to do. Earth owned Him. When His soul was offered, His glory was upon Him. He was a Prince and a Son to rule. . . . The mystery of God's greatness. Saints of God on earth. God's signs and wonders, witnesses of His glory and return.

Charles Harrison Mason,
"An Exhortative Invocation" (1919),
taken from *Conversations with God:
Two Centuries of Prayers by African-Americans*

CHAPTER EIGHT

O Stands for "Open Up!"

*H*op On!
Open Up!
*P*ray Back!
*E*nter In!

William Pannell, professor of preaching and world-renowned African-American Christian leader, observes that after years of trying to find ways to communicate *beyond* the biblical text, many churches are returning to the simplicity of preaching *from* the text itself.[1] Messengers of hope couldn't be happier! Every message of hope goes back to the Word.

The Arsenal of Texts

Having set the stage through stories of God's ways in awakenings, it's time to aggressively open up for our hearers the biblical arsenal of texts. Revival reports aren't entertaining novelties to make us feel better. They are reinforcements of the biblical promises that point us toward spiritual revolution. God's Word alone can successfully prepare us for and take us through extraordinary seasons of grace.

Results of neglecting this second ingredient are tragically illustrated from recent genocide in Africa. Rwanda was the birthplace of what is known as the East African revival, beginning some five decades ago. That revival has spread throughout many parts of East Africa, impacting Rwanda so significantly that 85 percent of its population called itself "Christian" at the beginning of the 1990s. Rwanda hosted large evangelistic crusades, with record conversions between 1991 and 1993. So what went wrong? "Did God turn his back on Rwanda," as *Time* magazine claimed? What lessons has the church in Africa learned from this tragedy? Tokumboh Adeyemo answers his own questions this way: "Solid and sound biblical teaching did not follow to sustain the fire of revival. Instead, the church leaders were caught in the political game of ethnic rivalry and control of power."[2]

If God's agenda for revival and awakening is to prevail, there's an indisputable necessity for clear biblical teaching. How sad that a move of God in a nation so desperately in need of Christ's dramatic presence in the church was never fanned into full-blown, life-changing revival. Let us learn from this kind of revival story as well. Only a Christ-centered, Bible-based awakening has the power to sustain and change the world in the way God desires.

When Jonathan Edwards wrote a book calling for concerts of prayer in the thick of the First Great Awakening, he chose a lengthy title of nearly thirty-five words. It outlined the need to mobilize visible, explicit, united prayer for revival and missions. The final words of the title stated that all of this must be done "according to the prophecies and promises of the Holy Word of God." In a day of impending revival, Edwards insists, messengers of hope must open up God's "prophecies and promises" in a way that drives us to concerted prayer and to readiness for what is coming. Like Paul, every agent serves the church by fulfilling God's commission "to present to you the word of God *in its fullness* . . . to make known among the Gentiles the glorious riches of this mystery, which is Christ in you, the hope of glory. We proclaim him" (Col. 1:25–28).

Actually there are hundreds of passages from which to draw this message. For example, for nine months I scoured a copy of Scripture, working methodically from Genesis to Revelation, highlighting with a yellow pen every verse that demonstrates (either by promise, prophecy, or action) this fundamental claim: God is ready to do for us and to give us "immeasurably more than all we ask or imagine" (Eph. 3:20). When I finished the experiment, nearly half my Bible had turned yellow! No question about it: the Bible is *filled* with messages of hope. Most of them can also be related, directly or indirectly, to the hope of revival.

At the end of this chapter, I have listed twenty of what I consider to be some of the most potent biblical texts on the hope of revival. That can get you started. In another publication, *Biblical Agendas for Concerted Prayer,* I list hundreds of other texts that not only talk about the inward and outward dimensions of revival, but also point toward responses of repentance, spiritual warfare, zealous worship, and consecration of life, all filled with Christ-centered hope.[3]

Of course, certain books of the Bible brim with themes of hope such as Joshua, 2 Chronicles, Psalms, Isaiah, Zechariah (at least twelve separate messages on revival), Luke, Acts (a case study on an awakening), Ephesians (a blueprint of revival based on the massive breakthrough in Ephesus), as well as Hebrews and Revelation (which carries us into the final revival). Look for these and other passages to address topics such as:

The promises of God for revival
The ways of God in revival
The manifestations of God during revival
The impact of God on his people out of revival
The centrality of Christ in all revival
Personal and corporate dimensions of revival

If you do this, it won't be long before you have found enough messages of hope to keep you an active messenger until Christ's return!

Above all, as we saw earlier, every text on hope should summon our hearers to the feet of Christ. Remember the three key words (the major themes in every revival): *focus* on the person of Christ, the *fullness* of the life of Christ, the *fulfillment* of the mission of Christ. You may want to return to chapter 6 once more to study the questions at the end. See also the questions later in this chapter. By centering in on Christ, the questions will help you grasp even deeper ways to open up for others biblical teachings on revival.

Let's "Open Up!"

Ready to get started? Apply these practical guidelines as you involve your hearers in the second ingredient of every message of hope, opening up for them the biblical texts of revival.

Establish a Bridge

How is the text you want to teach from relevant to what you may have already told your hearers in your introductory highlights as you motivated them to "hop on"? Can you tie these first two ingredients to each other?

Establish a Theme

What is this specific text going to do for your hearers? How will the passage reveal to them God's character, ways, and promises in order to build in them a greater hope for personal, local, national, or even world revival? How will this text challenge them to be more fully prepared and involved when revival comes? Do you need to tell them this specifically before you read the passage?

Read the Text to Them

Read God's Word with the enthusiasm it deserves. Through it, God is giving your hearers extraordinary hope for themselves and their generation.

Establish the Context

Where does this passage fit within redemptive history? Or within a particular moment of redemptive history? Or within the immediate experience of God's people at the time it was written? Can you show your hearers any similarities between the context for this text and the spiritual challenges in our own times?

Unfold a Vision of Revival

You may want to use the following questions to dig out what the passage teaches. They will help you think through how to teach the passage to your audience for maximum clarity and motivation. There are many ways to approach your time of teaching, but here are a few suggestions.

How might this text, directly or indirectly, show in fresh ways how God manifests himself in times of renewal or revival? *(focus)*

How does this text help to better define the ways spiritual awakening gives God's people a healthier, deeper life together in him? *(fullness)*

How does this text speak, directly or indirectly, to the mission thrust of God's people toward one other person, a whole community, or an entire nation? What role does renewal and awakening play? *(fulfillment)*

What does this text teach about what it takes in any generation for God to unleash revival?

What does this text reveal about hindrances to revival (either inside or outside the church)?

What does this text teach about important steps we should take to prepare individually or corporately for a coming revival?

Are there supporting texts from other passages of Scripture that might be woven into your teaching on this text?

How might this text encourage your hearers to *expect* God to intervene with us in extraordinary ways, to accomplish much more than we have ever seen?

Using this text, how can you preach Christ more fully to your hearers as the one who guarantees and sums up all this text teaches on revival? As the one around whom awakening centers?

How would Christ be more central in the church's experience, and even among unbelievers, if this text would receive a much fuller expression in our generation?

How do the principles and activities of revival portrayed, defined, or promised in this passage point us, in anticipation, to the final revival at the end of history? What will it be like for every hope highlighted in this text to find its consummation in the day of Christ's coming? How should that change the way you depict the unleashing of "approximations" of the promises for your hearers right now, right where they live?

Promote Anticipation

Stir their imaginations. Challenge them to imagine what it might look like if God were to do in our time what this passage promises.

Ask them if they can be satisfied to go on living with anything less than blessings like these from God. Is this what God desires? What he deserves?

Reaffirm your own confidence that such a work of God in revival is at hand; that he is not only able and willing but also *ready* to do it.

Tell a concluding story from past or present demonstrations of revival to illustrate the central hope of this text.

In all that you share, be both personal and passionate.

Make the Text Your Own

Finally, the text must also be lodged deep in the messenger's soul, not just his brain. As David Allen Hubbard taught so often, "Apply your whole self to the text; apply the whole text to yourself. Trust God for the results."[4] This is foundational to infusing your audience with a message of hope. Heralds—parents, Sunday school teachers, pastors—need to spend time in God's presence to receive God's message. Only a message that comes that way will open up hearts to believe God for "great and unsearchable things you do not know" (Jer. 33:3).

Can we anticipate *immediate* results if we are faithful to open up the Bible in these ways? Absolutely! First of all, faith comes by hearing (Rom. 10:17). Therefore, every message of hope activates stronger levels of faith toward God. We give our hearers a whole new way to think about God and about their daily walk with Christ. They receive from us exciting perspectives to transform their own studies of Scrip-

ture in the weeks ahead. Since faith is the evidence of things hoped for (Heb. 11:1), as hope grows so does faith. Everything else in the Christian life flows out of faith. So results *will* be immediate. Taken captive to the whole counsel of God, Christians can't help but be transformed into prisoners of hope. As the vision is substantiated with the Word of God, your hearers will be set free from fears—fears of being disappointed or fears of the cost of revival. Greater confidence to prepare for revival—and more insights on how to do so—will explode with joyful anticipation.

When the church begins to throb with people like this, in a sense revival has already begun! Now, more than ever, they're ready to pray.

Twenty Passages That "Open Up" Revival

I promised to end with Scriptures that I've enjoyed using. This is just the beginning:

Old Testament

1 Samuel 7:2–15
2 Samuel 5:1–12
2 Chronicles 7:11–16
2 Chronicles 15:1–15
Psalm 80
Psalm 102:1–22
Isaiah 59:15–60:3
Jeremiah 33:1–22
Joel 2:12–32
Haggai 2:1–9

New Testament

Luke 1:68–79
Luke 2:25–38
Luke 3:1–9, 15–18
Acts 4:23–35
Acts 19:1–20
Romans 11:11–16
Ephesians 1:15–23
Ephesians 3:14–21
1 Thessalonians 1:2–10
Revelation 3:14–22

Father, thou openeth the gates of wonders, making us enjoy the gift of the Christ, his word standing. When the wicked comes against us the power of thy word is for us.

Open the gates of thy wisdom for us and rebuke the power of the wicked against us. In the glory of Thy council we stand. The Christ of thy word has made us stand.

We see the door of thy mystery. Let the poor confess their sins and see the glory of thy resurrection. Thy goodness and greatness is among the daughters. Fill these with the fullness of Christ. Bless us with light and prudence in the power of the Holy Ghost. The presence of God is with us and the blood prevails. Anoint us so we will in Thy pity come to thee.

Charles Harrison Mason,
"An Exhortative Invocation" (1919),
taken from *Conversations with God:
Two Centuries of Prayers by African-Americans*

CHAPTER NINE

P STANDS FOR "PRAY BACK!"

*H*op On!
*O*pen Up!
Pray Back!
*E*nter In!

In the midst of a spiritual awakening, Martin Luther exclaimed, "I judge that my prayer is more than the devil himself; if it were otherwise, Luther would have fared differently long before this. If I should neglect prayer but a single day, I should lose a good deal of the fire of faith."[1] That's how seriously every Messenger of Hope must define prayer; it is key to the success of his or her calling. This is true not only for us but for our hearers as well. We must constantly help those with whom we share our message of hope to pray that message back to God, asking him to translate the message into reality, according to his Word. Prayer is the first and primary response to a message of hope; it also completes the message. It keeps the fire of faith (and hope) burning.

This was illustrated during the huge prayer rally I guided in Hong Kong Stadium, when we asked God to use the return of Hong Kong rule to mainland China as a vehicle to bring revival. As I explained in the introduction of this book, we centered our thinking on Jeremiah 33:3: "Call to me and I will answer you and tell you great and unsearchable things you do not know." Then I walked this gathering through nearly three hours of prayer using the whole thirty-third chapter. In this passage, the prophet describes a city awash in revival. I asked the thousands before me to envision what it would look like for God to reproduce Jeremiah 33 within Hong Kong, especially after 1997. What a powerful experience we had that hot July afternoon, praying back to God the great and unsearchable things revealed so long ago. Hope blazed!

Why pray? Why is this a key ingredient for every message of hope? Because Messengers of Hope leave their hearers with two unshakable conclusions: (1) This vision is too wonderful to live without, and (2) this vision is too wonderful to produce by ourselves. Our only alternative, therefore, is to seek divine intervention, to ask for the extraordinary. The more we pray like this, the more the flames of confidence spread, and the closer to revival we move.

Pray Back Together

Messengers of Hope also get God's people praying *together*. In previous revivals, these gatherings were called "concerts of prayer"—which meant concerted, united, corporate prayer. In point of fact, about 90 percent of what the Bible teaches on prayer is about corporate prayer. The hope that we proclaim is not just for an individual here or there. Most biblical promises for revival boast corporate manifestations. Ever since writing *Concerts of Prayer*, I have worked extensively with united prayer movements around the world. After twenty years, I've concluded that helping Christians join together to "pray back" the message of hope to God may actually be the single most important contribution made by any Messenger of Hope. Not only do such times of prayer allow God to initiate the fulfillment of the message, but it also provides time for immediate application of the Scriptures by the hearers in their prayers.

Pray Back Pointers

As you move your hearers into this third ingredient of praying God's message of hope back to him, keep these pointers in mind. Remember, they are equally applicable to family devotions, Sunday morning worship, or concerts of prayer.

Emphasize that the first and primary response to the message they've just heard is to intercede with God for its fulfillment. Show them the urgency of seeking God, of responding while the message is fresh. Praying needs to happen *now*.

Help them develop a strategic prayer agenda. Ask them questions like: What must God do for us *here* to reenact this passage or fulfill this promise in our experience? What would it look like? How might we be involved? As a result of such vision, what do we need to say to God, to seek him today for all that this hope offers us? (You might even provide them a few initial answers of your own, based on the text.) Then, help them express their insights in prayer to the Father.

Your prayer time may involve a combination of approaches. We want to avoid making anyone feel awkward or confused over how best to pray. Here are some successful approaches that you may adapt for your prayer time: Have your hearers pray your message back to God, working through major ideas in your message, praying verse by verse, or section by section. Encourage them to start off with a brief session in small groups, praying for two minutes over each verse or point. Interrupt at the end of each two minutes to summarize the next point and refocus them on the topic for the next two minutes.

Guide them in prayer through the three major facets of revival—focus, fullness, fulfillment—by drawing on what you taught them about each theme from the specific text just shared. A logical flow exists in moving in our thoughts from focus to fulfillment. Your prayer time could follow the sequencing of these three words, helping your hearers unpack even greater insights on revival as they reconstitute your message into these three categories. You might have them try five minutes apiece in small groups on each theme.

Or, from a very different direction, have them respond to your total message by working through what I call the six biblical responses of prayer. Described in greater detail elsewhere,[2] let me summarize them here:

Reflect—You might begin with a short period of silent prayer, thinking over the message and individually praying about its personal and corporate applications.

Rejoice—Next, direct a time of praising God for any prospects or promises the passage offers us or our generation. Also, praise him for all we have learned from the text about the person of Christ as the heart of revival. "Rejoice in the hope of the glory of God" (Rom. 5:2) remains one of the strongest expressions of worship. Praise God in anticipation of what is coming and the glory that revival will bring to his Son.

Repent—Here, address any personal or corporate hindrances to the revival highlighted by the text that might grieve or quench the Holy Spirit and so impede awakening. Repentance praying expresses our readiness to *turn away* from whatever in us contradicts the message of hope, and to *turn toward* everything Christ is offering us through the message of hope.

Resist—Together in prayer deal with hindrances and strongholds raised up from the outside by the powers of the Evil One. Often the chosen text will pinpoint certain battle lines God's people must face in God-given awakenings and the advance of Christ's kingdom. Through our prayers of resistance, we stand victorious over the forces of darkness, even before revival comes.

Request—Boldly seize upon the many promises held out in the text. Aggressively ask God to bring to pass in our own experience—in our churches, in our generation, even among the nations—all that the passage has revealed about Christ-centered awakening.

Recommit—All good revival praying will conclude by affirming deeper commitments to God. Encourage those praying to make a promise to continue praying like this until revival comes, to prepare for his work of revival through personal and corporate changes, and to be themselves an answer to their prayers, no

matter what it may cost. A time of rededication at the end of the prayers also predisposes hearers to the fourth ingredient of every message of hope, the call to "enter in" to revival right now.

In conducting concerted prayer, many additional approaches can be used to insure a positive prayer time for your hearers. Concerts of Prayer International, for example, offers a handbook titled *Creative Approaches to Concerts of Prayer* with over fifty suggestions.[3] In one of these suggestions, a team of leaders might model from the front how to pray point by point, or verse by verse, each taking thirty seconds apiece, one after the other. Or, a responsive prayer can be written out ahead of time, printed on a flyer, and used by everyone in the group to pray the message back to God.

I remember one time preaching about the revival under Elijah on Mount Carmel and concluding with a five-minute prayer that highlighted the drama. I asked the audience to respond after each summary point in my prayer by simultaneously whispering to God (with a sense of awe): "Let the fire fall!" None of those present will ever see 1 Kings 18 in the same way again.

A Challenge

Although anyone can be a Messenger of Hope, allow me a special word of challenge to pastors. For the next eight weeks, deliver a message of hope series on Sunday mornings. As an experiment, shorten your usual message time by ten minutes. Then assist your congregation to use that ten minutes to pray your message back to God.

How might you fill the "pray back" time? One possibility: At the end of the message, put people in groups of six (having them stand, with three people in one pew turning to face three in another). Six is a minimally threatening group size because at least three will be ready and willing to pray brief prayers out loud.

For the first minute, stand in silence, reflecting on or praising God for what has been heard. Use the next eight minutes to go over your major points, allowing two minutes for each point, praying in groups of six throughout the sanctuary. Encourage prayers of repentance, resistance, or request. Encourage prayer for yourselves, but also for your church, and beyond your walls. The final minute might be another time of silence for personal recommitment. Or, it could involve a corporate prayer—asking Christ to allow you to be part of God's answers to the previous nine minutes, using, perhaps, a responsive prayer you've composed ahead of time and placed in the bulletin.

Can we expect immediate results from this third ingredient? Of course! In a number of ways:

- *It will change the way you share your message.* Knowing that your hearers will take whatever you say and turn it into prayer, asking God to manifest what you have taught them through revival in their lives and in the lives of others, you'll be more dedicated to the preparation of your teaching and more enthusiastic to teach than ever before.

- *It will change the way they listen.* If they know the moment you've delivered the message they will be asked to pray it back to God, they might even take notes for a change! The hearers will actually join you in shaping the message, expanding, deepening, and applying the message by *how* they pray. Also, the prayer time will create a fresh environment for hearing, embracing, and obeying this message of hope. No better way exists for your listeners to lay hold of a vision for revival than by praying it back to God. As we pray, the Holy Spirit is able to get the message out of our heads and down into our hearts as never before.

- *It will change how your hearers apply the message.* The praying prepares them for ingredient four—to *"enter in"*—and for what your message calls them to expect and prepare for, day by day.

- *It will change the life of your church and the world beyond.* Why? Because we serve a God who answers prayer. When we ask something according to his will, he does it (1 John 5:14–15)! Praying back his Word to him means you are praying with certainty that you are seeking his will. In most cases your message will inspire your hearers to offer up to God prayers they have

never offered to him before. God will take full advantage of such an opportunity! Nothing can remain the same.

Yes, Luther is right. Prayer secures the fire of hope. It also secures every message of hope. In the end, it transforms hearers into prisoners of hope. Like Jacob of old, full of hope that Abraham's covenant blessing was about to fall on him, they will not let go until they see God's face (compare Gen. 32:26–30 with 33:10–11).

These signs follow believers. The people receiving the Holy Ghost have something which the world cannot understand. The comforter proceeding from the Father going on in us, and through us. Earth testify to the shortage of the Church, knowing nothing of the greatness of God. All praise to God. Having found the faith, baptized in Him, I'm telling the story of Him. He is God for you. He is God to do. He is your thrilling life, the only help now we show. Pouring upon us the help of His power and love. Accept Him in might, saying God is right. Ask the Lord for help the more. Looking for God to guide the soul.

Charles Harrison Mason,
"An Exhortative Invocation" (1919),
taken from *Conversations with God:*
Two Centuries of Prayers by African-Americans

CHAPTER TEN

E Stands for "Enter In!"

*H*op On!
*O*pen Up!
*P*ray Back!
Enter In!

A respected African-American pastor led a revival prayer rally in Chicago, with almost two thousand in attendance from across the city. He asked us to respond to his prayer with the same response as another messenger of hope, Isaiah: "Here am I, Lord! Send me!" His request seemed rather innocent. As he began, he prayed first for God's work in our own lives, and then in our churches. We responded to each prayer: "Here am I, Lord! Send me!" Next he spoke to God about some of the desperate needs of the city. At the end of a brief petition for each concern—addressing the unrelenting battles of the poor and the homeless, praying for those abandoned in prisons and those with AIDS, calling for revival within the political establishment—we announced, "Here am I, Lord! Send me!" Finally his prayers swept on to the extensive challenge of sharing the gospel with specific unreached people groups across the globe. Still we joined him to conclude each intercession with, "Here am I, Lord! Send me!"

In essence, we were giving God carte blanche to send us anywhere at any price to be an answer to our own prayers. As his twelve-minute prayer unfolded, you could feel the audience responses dwindling in energy, more and more muffled—I would even call it timid. We were all waking up to the implications of seeking God for revival. Were we really *that* eager to enter into it if God would grant it?

In fact, no message of hope is complete until we have called prisoners of hope to active participation in the unleashing of their vision—to be the answer to their prayers, to prepare themselves for all that revival will call them into for Christ's sake, and to start acting as if revival is coming.

The Risk of Being Shaken

In typical British understatement, J. B. Phillips writes: "Anyone who opens his personality to the living Spirit of God takes the risk of being considerably shaken."[1] The same can be said of anyone who opens himself or herself to the Spirit's gift of hope. Are you willing to take such a risk? If so, are you convinced that you must also invite your hearers to let God considerably shake them too? This is the fourth ingredient in every message of hope. Each message must conclude with such a compelling ring of hope that we send people out to actively engage it in simple steps of preparation, living daily in anticipation of God doing exceedingly more in genuine revival. Our job is not done until we provide our hearers with practical "next steps" toward obedience as prisoners of hope.

If, in fact, we announce the promise of revival in the right ways, our hearers will stir with holy restlessness over the status quo. They will require us to help them move into new territory. So it is your job as a Messenger of Hope to exploit their longings by suggesting fresh ways to obey Christ. Christians must believe and act as if such a revival really is at hand, impending, bearing down on top of us. Teaching people to "enter in" isn't about *reactionary* living. New Testament discipleship, a proper response to every message of hope, is *anticipatory* discipleship. Faithfulness to Christ is lived out in anticipation of where he is headed and what more he is ready to do with us. To truly understand this important truth would turn almost every disciple-making curriculum in our churches upside-down. We're

moving from faith to faith, promise to promise, glory to glory (John 1:16; 3:34–35; Rom. 1:8, 17; 2 Cor. 3:17–18). Pouring out ourselves for Christ today gets us ready for the outpouring of his Spirit tomorrow.

Dealing in issues of practical living is similar to the ways Christians create seasons of spiritual preparations during Advent and Lent. In both, Christians are asked to practice living in a way that demonstrates anticipation of something more wonderful to come—the incarnation and passion of our Lord.

Messengers of Hope should reflect on the work of John the Baptist. John's message was straightforward: "Repent, for the kingdom of heaven is near" (Matt. 3:2). In other words, "Get ready. The King is about to break in upon you."

In the Book of Luke we read: "The word of God came to John son of Zechariah in the desert. . . . 'A voice of one calling in the desert, "Prepare the way for the Lord, make straight paths for him.""' . . . The people were waiting expectantly. . . . 'one more powerful than I will come, the thongs of whose sandals I am not worthy to untie. He will baptize you with the Holy Spirit and with fire'" (3:2, 4, 15–16). Then John called his hearers to very specific acts of anticipatory obedience, such as sharing with the poor and working for justice.

We can nurture no higher ambitions than to mobilize our hearers to wait expectantly, to take steps of repentance and change, and to be ready to "enter in" as revival comes. Isaiah states it well:

> Loose the chains of injustice and untie the cords of the yoke . . . set the oppressed free . . . share your food with the hungry and provide the poor wanderer with shelter. . . . Then your light will break forth like the dawn, and your healing will quickly appear. . . . Then you will call and the LORD will answer.
>
> Isaiah 58:6–9

Many texts outlining the church's preparations for the final revival (the consummation) have equal application to the attitude of any prisoner of hope longing to "enter in" to the work of revival. Take the words of Peter: "You ought to live holy and godly lives as you look forward to the day of God and speed its coming. . . . since you are looking forward to this, make every effort to be found spotless, blameless and at peace with him" (2 Peter 3:11–12, 14). Or again, follow the advice of John: "Continue in him, so that when he appears we may be confident and unashamed before him at his coming. . . . we know that when he appears, we shall be like him, for we shall see him as he is. Everyone who has this hope in him purifies himself, just as he is pure" (1 John 2:28; 3:2–3). Shouldn't the church be living in this atmosphere all the time—not only looking toward the consummation, but anticipating every approximation of the consummation when Christ appears in that powerful manifestation of his presence that generations have called revival? John Piper, one of our nation's leading pastors, has recently written 450 pages on what he calls "the purifying power of living by faith in Future Grace."[2]

How to "Enter In"

As you think of calling your hearers to "enter in" to the coming revival, you might want to answer for them one or more of the following questions, depending on what you've shared through the previous three ingredients:

How should we worship God more accurately in anticipation of the great works we believe he is getting ready to do? Also, in what ways does this vision require a change in our daily prayer life alone and together?

How will we begin to study the Scriptures differently on our own, as we look for themes of revival like those we just explored?

How should we adjust our lives together—as families, as small groups, as a church—so that we are ready to receive deeper visitations of the Holy Spirit when God is ready to grant them?

In what ways might we currently be grieving, quenching, or resisting the Spirit, either in our individual or corporate discipleship? Where is repentance required for moral sins? For unbelief? For indifference to spiritual opportunities? For ungodly distractions? For false hopes? For prayerlessness?

If, in fact, a fresh invasion of Christ by revival is just ahead of us, how would we reevaluate the extent and form of personal possessions? What needs to change in our giving patterns to the church, to ministries, to missions, to the poor?

In what way does this message give us new courage for evangelism? How can this message be incorporated into what we share with unbelievers when we tell them the good news of Christ? How can we share with them the stories of revival, for example, in ways that will entice them to take another look at who Christ is? How will this help prepare the way for a spiritual awakening to Christ?

Where do we need to work at racial or denominational reconciliation, especially locally, in anticipation of a revival God intends for the blessing of the whole body of Christ?

In light of the hope of coming revival, how do we need to readjust the weekly schedule and programming of our church? How can we reinvigorate our church activities so that this rising sense of hope is woven into all of them? How can we retool the disciple-making curriculum to be much more anticipatory in its focus?

Does this particular message of hope bring any adjustments to our social or political involvements? What social policies, for example, are most in keeping with what God will do in a national spiritual awakening to Christ? What political activities might contradict our claim for the need of divine intervention?

How does the coming revival impact the ways I look at world evangelization? Does this particular message of hope give me new courage to open my life to be sent by God, in the mission of Christ, in directions where I've not gone before?

If we succeed in asking listeners to "enter in" to the work of revival, once again we can anticipate immediate results from our ministry. How? More than ever before, our people will be better prepared for, less in the way of, and more likely candidates for God's visitation. The steps taken to prepare for revival cause us to "enter in" right now to richer levels of Christ-honoring discipleship (individually and corporately) than could be experienced otherwise. We will (to use John's words) purify ourselves because of the hope that's within us— hope for any imminent revival and the final revival.

Let me be clear here. None of this implies that we can somehow make revival happen if we simply take the correct steps. Rather, we *respond* to what God is about to do to bring revival to fruition. Renewed obedience springs from hope grounded in the sovereignty of God.

From Prisoners to Messengers

Whatever you do, as you lead others to obedience, pick out no more than one or two opportunities for application of a specific message. That's about all the change a person can handle at any one time. Also, be sure to give an illustration of what the application might look like. People need to see specific examples.

Without a doubt, one of the most important applications—one of the most strategic ways to "enter in" to God's work in coming revival—is to invite your hearers to be not only prisoners of hope, but also to become Messengers of Hope themselves. They, too, can begin to share this vision with other Christians on a regular basis. Encourage them to pass along the message you gave to them. Remember, the great need of the hour is to flood our nation with Messengers of Hope, agents of revival.

A significant step toward this goal is for your hearers to commit to be more intentional in their study of the topic of revival. One tool to help them is the small group discussion guide for *The Hope at Hand* called *Take It to Your Friends*.[3] Or, you can also use the ten-session study curriculum incorporated in *Stand in the Gap: How to Get Ready for the Coming World Revival*.[4]

Finally, to quicken their growth into Messengers of Hope, have your hearers consider forming a concert of prayer. As they gather with other prisoners of hope to pray for revival on a regular basis, even if just for a few minutes a week—maybe between Sunday school and worship—the message of hope they've heard from you will become a vision sought and shared. No better doorway exists for Christians who want to "enter in" to the coming revival.

Epilogue

Exalted or Exhausted?

One evening, a friend of mine acted as a Messenger of Hope during his family's devotions. He read the exciting story of the Spirit's coming on the day of Pentecost. He reported similarly surprising outreaches among Christian young people at a local high school. The family sang the chorus: "He is exalted; the King is exalted on high. I will praise him." Following Mom's brief prayer of commitment to the family's own witness the next day, my friend pointed his children toward bed. As he was climbing the stairs with his three-year-old in his arms, the boy began to sing the chorus once again. One word, however, got altered in the child's mind. He sang: "He is *exhausted;* the King is exhausted on high." My friend remarked to me later, "That really got me thinking! If Christ is not *exalted* in revival, the church will end up *exhausted* trying to do it for him."

That's the conviction of every Messenger of Hope. We must exalt Christ so he can do for us what we cannot possibly do for ourselves. This realization keeps us going. And we are exalting him by preaching a vision of Christ that is as comprehensive as all the promises of God. We do it with the confidence that he is ready to pour out fresh revelations of those promises on the very people with whom we share. Then he will be even more exalted. And we will turn from exhaustion to "times of refreshing" from the presence of the Lord (Acts 3:19).

What a reason to serve the kingdom! We bring people H.O.P.E. We enable other believers to:

Hop on—Get up to speed with what God has done and is doing in revival.

Open up—Help them to see in Scripture the ways and promises of God in revival.

Pray back—Lead them to seek God together for the fulfillment of this hope.

Enter in—Encourage them in steps of practical obedience to prepare the way for the coming revival.

Not long ago I met with six hundred pastors—Messengers of Hope—in Costa Rica. We devoted three days to strategizing about what it would take to complete the evangelization of their nation. We decided to set aside one afternoon to seek God about our plans. Just as we began to pray, it started raining. The building was covered with a tin roof, however. So the pounding torrent made it impossible to hear even the person next to you. For most of that prayer meeting we had to sit in personal silence, listening to the rain, pondering for an hour what the Spirit was saying to each of our hearts—alone in the storm, as it were, with God.

My thoughts wandered to John on the Isle of Patmos. I recalled how he fell at Jesus' feet in similar silence, like a dead man, overwhelmed by the magnitude of Christ's glory and power. And yet it was there, in the silence, that John received one of the greatest messages of hope ever sent, not only for the churches of Asia (see Acts 2 and 3) but for the whole body of Christ in the twenty-first century.

Cradled in showers outside San Jose, Costa Rica, many pastors were being similarly prepared by God, in silence, to be Messengers of Hope. Those moments were far more important for Christ's kingdom than all the strategies we had concocted during the previous days of deliberations.

Like America, like every nation, Costa Rica's greatest need is to be flooded with Messengers of Hope. Either Christ is exalted—by what we herald, what we pray, and what we receive in true revival—or our work for God will finally collapse in exhaustion. In your role as a parent, a student, pastor, doctor, business leader, missionary, choir director, or whatever, I ask you: Can there be any higher calling than this, to be a Messenger of Hope? Does there exist a more sacred privilege?

Who will volunteer as an agent of revival to follow the Holy Spirit as *the* Agent of Revival? Because revival *is* coming . . . it is "the hope at hand." He *will* be exalted!

Hear God's summons to another Messenger of Hope; it is for you as well:

Look at the nations and watch—and be utterly amazed. For I am going to do something in your days that you would not believe, even if you were told. . . .

Write down the revelation and make it plain on tablets so that a herald may run with it. For the revelation awaits an appointed time; it speaks of the end and will not prove false. Though it linger, wait for it; it will certainly come and will not delay. . . . For the earth will be filled with the knowledge of the glory of the LORD, as the waters cover the sea.

LORD, I have heard of your fame; I stand in awe of your deeds, O LORD. Renew them in our day, in our time make them known; in wrath remember mercy.

Habakkuk 1:5; 2:2–3, 14; 3:2

NOTES

Introduction: *The Operative Word Is* Hope

1. David Bryant, *The Hope at Hand: National and World Revival for the Twenty-First Century* (Grand Rapids: Baker, 1995). This volume is the companion book to *Messengers of Hope* and provides background on revival and the current developments toward revival that I have not taken time to study in depth in this book.

2. Contact Concerts of Prayer International for a catalog on a variety of books and resources (P.O. Box 1399, Wheaton, IL 60189). Ask for *Engaging God Together: Distinctive Resources for Mobilizing God's People to Pray.* Also, see my foundational book, recently revised, *Concerts of Prayer: Christians Join for Spiritual Awakening and World Evangelization* (Ventura, Calif.: Regal, 1986, 1997).

3. Pope John Paul II, *Crossing the Threshold of Hope* (New York: Knopf, 1995).

4. Dietrich Bonhoeffer, *Creation and Fall* (New York: Collier, 1959), 11.

5. A statement by historian Paul Toyer, quoted in Wendy Murray Zoba, "Future Tense: How Do We Live under the Shadow of 'The End'?" *Christianity Today,* 2 October 1995, 20.

6. A term coined by David Neff, senior editor for *Christianity Today,* in an editorial "Why Hope Is a Virtue," *Christianity Today,* 3 April 1995, 24.

7. Eugene H. Peterson, *Reversed Thunder: The Revelation of John and the Praying Imagination* (San Francisco: HarperSanFrancisco, 1988), 9.

8. Christian social critic Richard John Neuhaus, quoted in Neff, "Why Hope Is a Virtue," 24.

9. Quoted in the video *John Wycliffe: The Morning Star,* produced by Vanguard Video, a Division of United Entertainment, Inc.; from the Vision Video collection.

10. Christian Furhrer quoted in Barbara von der Heydt, "Has the Salt Lost Its Saltiness in Leipzig?" *World,* 5 October 1996, 22.

11. Martyn Lloyd-Jones, *Joy Unspeakable: Power and Renewal in the Holy Spirit* (Wheaton: Harold Shaw, 1984), 16. See also the Lloyd-Jones volume, *Revival* (Westchester, Ill.: Crossway, 1987), in which similar understandings are discussed in greater depth.

12. Martyn Lloyd-Jones, *Faith: Tried and Triumphant,* quoted in the "Reflections" section of *Christianity Today,* 18 July 1994, 45.

13. Alister McGrath, "Why Evangelicalism Is the Future of Protestantism," *Christianity Today,* 19 June 1995, 22.

14. Leighton Ford, "A Letter to Future Leaders," *Christianity Today*, 11 November 1996, 17.

15. John Piper, *The Pleasures of God: Meditations on the Delight of God in Being God* (Portland, Ore.: Multnomah, 1991), 206. For a more popularized writing on the topic of hope in the Christian life, I also suggest Don Hawkins, *Never Give Up* (Lincoln: Back to the Bible Publishers, 1992).

16. Henri J. Nouwen, quoted in the "Reflections" section of *Christianity Today*, 11 November 1996, 81.

17. Peterson, *Reversed Thunder*, 154.

18. Philip Yancey, *Disappointment with God: Three Questions No One Asks Aloud* (Grand Rapids: Zondervan, 1988), 201.

19. Stephen L. Carter, *The Culture of Disbelief: How American Law and Politics Trivialize Religious Devotion* (New York: Anchor Books/Doubleday, 1993), 60.

20. Jonathan Kozol, *Amazing Grace: The Lives of Children and the Conscience of a Nation* (New York: Crown Publishers, 1995).

21. Bishop George McKinney, quoted in Andreas Tapia, "Soul Searching: How Is the Black Church Responding to the Urban Crisis?" *Christianity Today*, 4 March 1996, 30.

22. Tony Evans, *Are Christians Destroying America? How to Restore a Decaying Culture* (Chicago: Moody, 1996), 28.

23. Samuel D. Proctor, *The Substance of Things Hoped For: A Memoir of African-American Faith* (New York: G. P. Putnam's Sons, 1995), quoted in Barbara Reynolds, "That River of Faith Can Still Turn the Tide," *USA Today*, 3 February 1996, 19.

24. The prayers quoted throughout this book are taken from James Melvin Washington, *Conversations with God: Two Centuries of Prayers by African-Americans* (New York: HarperCollins, 1995).

25. David Bryant, *Stand in the Gap: How to Get Ready for the Coming World Revival*, rev. ed. (Ventura, Calif.: Regal, 1997). See especially chapter 3, "Retreating from the Gap: The Curse of Pea-Sized Christianity." The book itself was written to deliver the reader from limited perspectives on Christ and his mission to the world, so that we might be better prepared to join in the coming revival as God grants it.

Chapter 1: *A Nation in Need of Messengers of Hope*

1. The full text of Dr. Graham's message was published in the Intercessors for America newsletter, September 1996, 1–3.

2. Bill Gates, *The Road Ahead* (New York: Viking Press, 1995).

3. Carl F. H. Henry, "No Wine before Its Time," *World*, 6 January 1996, 30.

4. Luis Palau, *The Only Hope for America* (Wheaton: Crossway, 1996), 49.

5. Quoted by Chuck Colson in "The Upside of Pessimism," *Christianity Today*, 15 August 1995, 64.

6. David B. Barrett, "Living in the World of A.D. 2000," *World Evangelization*, November/December 1988, 11.

7. "Breaking Point," an in-depth report appearing in *Newsweek*, 6 March 1995, 56–61.

8. See Robert Right, "The Evolution of Despair," *Time*, 28 August 1995, 50–57.

9. A 1996 national Gallup survey.

10. Jürgen Moltmann, writing in and reviewed by *Theology News and Notes*, Fuller Theological Seminary (19 October 1996). See Jürgen Moltmann, "Theology in Modern Society," and Winston E. Gooden, "Theology, Crises, and Modern Values."

11. For a complete discussion on this issue see James Davison Hunter, *Before the Shooting Begins: Searching for Democracy in America's Culture War* (New York: Free Press, 1994).

12. See interview with John Leo, "Counter Punch Morality," *Christianity Today,* 7 October 1996, 62.

13. Robert H. Bork, *Slouching towards Gomorrah: Modern Liberalism and American Decline* (New York: HarperCollins, 1996), 11.

14. See a fuller discussion by Jeff Greenfield, "Voter Anxiety: A Chronic Condition," *Time,* 22 April 1996, 58.

15. For a thorough discussion on these concepts see Michael Medved, "Protecting Our Children from a Plague of Pessimism," *Imprimis* (a publication of Hillsdale College, Michigan) (19 December 1995): 1–7.

16. See a thorough discussion on this understanding of hope in George Barna, *The Power of Vision: How to Capture and Apply God's Vision for Your Ministry* (Ventura, Calif.: Regal, 1992).

17. Cal Thomas, "The Sixties Are Dead; Long Live the Nineties," *Imprimis* (January 1995): 1.

18. Chuck Colson in a forum/interview "One Lord, One Voice?" *Christianity Today,* 7 October 1996, 39.

19. Colson, "Upside of Pessimism," 64.

20. Aleksandr Solzhenitsyn first used the metaphor "spiritual exhaustion" in his 1978 Harvard commencement address.

21. Taken from the survey entitled "How Teenagers See Things," *Parade,* 18 August 1996, 4.

22. Douglas Coupland, *Life after God* (New York: Pocket Books, 1994), 359.

23. The term "generation of seekers" is taken from Wade Clark Roof, *A Generation of Seekers: Spiritual Journeys of the Baby Boomer Generation* (San Francisco: HarperSanFrancisco, 1994).

24. For a fuller discussion see "In Search of the Sacred," *Newsweek,* 28 November 1994, 52–62.

25. Shirley Dobson is quoted in a news report on the 1996 National Day of Prayer, *National and International Religion Report* 10, no. 11 (13 May 1996): 3.

26. John D. Beckett, "Things I'm Thinking: On the Eve of the November Elections," Intercessors for America newsletter, November 1996, 2.

27. Jacques Ellul, *Hope in Time of Abandonment* (New York: Seabury Press, 1973), 27.

28. J. I. Packer, "Our Lifeline: The Bible Is the Rope God Throws Us," *Christianity Today,* 28 October 1996, 22.

29. George Barna, *Absolute Confusion: How Our Moral and Spiritual Foundations Are Eroding in This Age of Change* (Ventura, Calif.: Regal, 1994), 138.

30. Bork, *Slouching towards Gomorrah,* 331, 343.

Chapter 2: *Messengers of Hope, Agents of Revival*

1. From an interview with Tokumboh Adeyemo entitled "Africa: The Light Continent?" by Stan Guthrie, Evangelical Missions Information Service, *World Pulse* 31, no. 2 (19 January 1996): 1.

2. George Barna, *Turnaround Churches: How to Overcome Barriers to Growth and Bring New Life to an Established Church* (Ventura, Calif.: Regal, 1993), 50.

3. See the complete treatment by William Strauss and Neil Howe, *The Fourth Turning* (New York: Broadway, 1997). The authors also present a good summary of their thesis in the article "What's Next?" *USA Today,* 27–29 December 1996, 4–5.

4. David Bryant, *The Hope at Hand: National and World Revival for the Twenty-First Century* (Grand Rapids: Baker, 1995), 16.

5. "Entire City Pauses for Prayer, Even at High Tide of Business," *Denver Post,* 20 January 1905, 1.

6. Iain H. Murray, *The Puritan Hope: A Study of Revival and the Interpretation of Prophecy* (Carlisle, Pa.: The Banner of Truth Trust, 1971), 90, 112, 127–28.

7. Robert H. Fogle, "The Fourth Great Awakening," *Wall Street Journal,* 9 January 1996, 7.

8. George Barna presented this analysis during a seminar in Nashville on 19 February 1996. It was reported in *National and International Religion Report* 10, no. 7 (18 March 1996): 1.

9. The video *Get Ready: Christian Leaders Speak Out on the Coming Revival* is produced by the National Prayer Committee. It is available, among other sources, from Concerts of Prayer International, P.O. Box 1399, Wheaton, IL 60189.

10. Erwin W. Lutzer, "America's Spiritual Crisis," *Revival Commentary* (fall 1996): 12.

11. Os Guinness, "Mission in the Face of Modernity," *World Evangelization,* January 1990, 10.

12. Os Guinness, "William Bennett's 'Spiritual Despair': Is America in Revolt against God?" *Policy Review* (spring 1994): 44.

13. Billy Graham, "America Sees a Spiritual Awakening," *U.S. News and World Report,* 25 December 1995, 85.

14. Michael Cromartie, "Conquering the Enemy Within: An Interview with Economist Glenn Loury," *Christianity Today,* 8 January 1996, 20.

15. Ralph D. Winter, "Let No One Scoff at What God Can Do!" *Mission Frontiers Bulletin,* May/June 1995, 6.

16. From an article on John Stott by David Wells entitled "Guardian of God's Word," *Christianity Today,* 16 September 1996, 54.

17. John Piper, *The Supremacy of God in Preaching* (Grand Rapids: Baker, 1990), 108–9.

18. George Barna, in the third of the video training series by Gospel Light entitled *Turning Vision into Action,* quoted in *Leadership* (winter 1997): 111.

19. Taken from *Hope for Europe: An Initiative of the European Round Table,* produced by the European Evangelical Alliance and the Lausanne European Committee, 19 December 1994, 8.

Chapter 3: *Turn Fellow Christians into Prisoners of Hope*

1. See further discussion on "prisoners of hope" in chapter 6 of David Bryant, *Stand in the Gap: How to Get Ready for the Coming World Revival,* rev. ed. (Ventura, Calif.: Regal, 1997).

2. The phrase "urban Pentecost" was coined by Ray Bakke, president of International Urban Associates, Chicago.

3. Taken from William Muehl, *Why Preach? Why Listen?* (Minneapolis: Fortress, 1986), and referred to by Martin E. Marty in *Context: A Commentary on the Interaction of Religion and Culture* 27, no. 8 (15 April 1995): 1.

4. William D. Hendricks, *Exit Interviews: Revealing Stories of Why People Are Leaving the Church* (Chicago: Moody, 1993).

5. Taken from a book review by Gordon MacDonald entitled "The Church's MIA's," *Christianity Today,* 16 May 1994, 57.

6. See the in-depth analysis by Leith Anderson in *A Church for the Twenty-First Century* (Minneapolis: Bethany, 1993).

7. George Barna, *Absolute Confusion: How Moral and Spiritual Foundations Are Eroding in This Age of Change* (Ventura, Calif.: Regal, 1994), 19.

8. George Barna, *Today's Pastors: A Revealing Look at What Pastors Are Saying about Themselves, Their Peers, and the Pressures They Feel* (Ventura, Calif.: Regal, 1993), 91.

9. See interview with John Leo, "Counter Punch Morality," *Christianity Today,* 7 October 1996, 63.

10. Tony Evans, *Are Christians Destroying America?: How to Restore a Decaying Culture* (Chicago: Moody, 1996), 18.

11. David Bryant, *Stand in the Gap: How to Prepare for the Coming World Revival* (Ventura, Calif.: Regal, 1997), chap. 6.

12. See discussion on "Predisposition toward the Status Quo" in David Bryant, *The Hope at Hand: National and World Revival for the Twenty-First Century* (Grand Rapids: Baker, 1995), 102–13, 211–15.

13. David B. Barrett, "Do We Have Adequate Resources to Evangelize the World?" *World Evangelization,* March/April 1989, 21.

14. George Barna, *Today's Pastors,* 66, 101.

15. From a paper presented by Paul McKaughan, president of the Evangelical Fellowship of Mission Agencies (EFMA), at their annual meeting in September 1994, entitled *Is There a Crisis in Missionary Motivation and Support?*

16. Graham Kendrick, "Shine, Jesus, Shine" (London: Make Way Publishers, 1987).

17. Noted in the 1993 research project for *See You at the Pole,* conducted by the Barna Research Group, October 1993, for the National Network of Youth Ministries.

18. For a thorough discussion of Zechariah 8, see chapter 3, "Anatomy of a Movement of Prayer," in David Bryant, *Concerts of Prayer: Christians Join for Spiritual Awakening and World Evangelization,* rev. ed. (Ventura, Calif.: Regal, 1997).

19. From John Calvin, *Instruction in Faith,* quoted by Martin E. Marty in *Context: A Commentary on the Interaction of Religion and Culture* 25, no. 8 (15 April 1995): 6.

20. See Bryant, *Hope at Hand,* chapter 10, "The Determined People."

21. Jacques Ellul, *Hope in Time of Abandonment* (New York: Seabury Press, 1973), 261.

Chapter 4: *The Confidence to Be a Messenger of Hope*

1. Taken from a survey by International Urban Associates (Chicago) and published in their IUA newsletter (winter 1994), 5.

2. W. Terry Whalin, "Faithful Bolivian Evangelist Gunned Down in Columbia," *New Man,* June 1996, 17.

3. E. M. Bounds, *Christian Advocate,* December 1890, quoted in *Glimpses* 65, an occasional publication of the Church History Institute.

4. For further discussion on the "tentative spirit" see David Bryant, *The Hope at Hand: National and World Revival for the Twenty-First Century* (Grand Rapids: Baker, 1995), 62–64.

5. George Barna, *Today's Pastors: A Revealing Look at What Pastors Are Saying about Themselves, Their Peers, and the Pressures They Feel* (Ventura, Calif.: Regal, 1993), 134–35.

6. Jim Reapsome, "Protection from What?" Evangelical Missions Information Service, *World Pulse* (15 December 1996): 8.

7. Lewis B. Smedes, "Forgiving God," *Theology News and Notes*, Fuller Theological Seminary (June 1996): 14.

8. Ebenezer Porter, *Letters on Revivals* (1830; reprint, Minneapolis: the Evangelical Free Church, 1993), 173.

9. Leith Anderson, *Decade of Volatility: Ten Powerful Trends Facing the Church*, special publication of the *National and International Religion Report* (February 1991): 18.

10. Richard Loveless, *Dynamics of Spiritual Life: An Evangelical Theology of Renewal* (Downers Grove, Ill.: InterVarsity Press, 1979), 424.

11. From a survey conducted by the Evangelistic Association of New England, published by the association in October 1994.

12. David L. Goetz, "Forced Out: A Summary of *Leadership*'s National Survey," *Leadership* (winter 1996): 42.

13. For a further exploration of these confidence builders see part 2 of Bryant, *Hope at Hand* entitled "The Surging Confidence." Each chapter deals with one of the confidence builders.

14. Taken from an interview by Edward Gilbreath entitled "The Pulpit King: The Passion and Eloquence of Gardner Taylor, a Legend among Preachers," *Christianity Today*, 11 December 1995, 28.

Chapter 5: *H.O.P.E.—Key Ingredients in Every Message of Hope*

1. Annie Dillard, *Teaching a Stone to Talk*, quoted in the "Reflections" section of *Christianity Today*, 12 August 1996, 48.

2. George Barna, "The Pulpit-Meister: Preaching to the New Majority," *Preaching*, January/February 1997, 12.

3. Taken from an interview with Bob Buford entitled "Helping the Successful Become Significant: How to Pastor the Powerful," *Leadership* (winter 1996): 122.

Chapter 6: *Christ: The Heart of the Message of Hope*

1. C. S. Lewis, *The Silver Chair* (New York: Collier, 1953), 17–18.

2. Mother Teresa, *The Simple Path* (New York: Ballantine Books, 1995).

3. Frederick Dale Bruner, "The Interpreter Spirit and the Current Crisis of the Church: An Exposition of John 16:7–11," *reNEWS*, a journal published by Presbyterians for Renewal (PCUSA), May 1994, 8.

4. Michael Horton, *In the Face of God: The Dangers and Delights of Spiritual Intimacy* (Dallas: Word, 1996), 169.

5. This idea was first suggested to me by Jim Reapsome in his editorial "Unspeakable Affront," Evangelical Missions Information Service, *World Pulse* (4 October 1996): 8.

6. Robert E. Webber, *The Majestic Tapestry: How the Power of Early Christian Tradition Can Enrich Contemporary Faith* (Nashville: Thomas Nelson, 1986), 24.

7. Philip Yancey, "Unwrapping Jesus: My Top Ten Surprises," *Christianity Today*, 17 June 1996, 34.

8. John R. W. Stott, *The Cross of Christ* (Downers Grove, Ill.: InterVarsity Press, 1986), 347.

9. David Bryant, *The Hope at Hand: National and World Revival for the Twenty-First Century* (Grand Rapids: Baker, 1995), 74.

10. Stephen L. Carter, *The Culture of Disbelief: How American Law and Politics Trivialize Religious Devotion* (New York: Anchor Books/Doubleday, 1993), 22–23.

11. See Donald W. McCullough, *The Trivialization of God: The Dangerous Illusion of a Manageable Deity* (Colorado Springs: NavPress, 1995).

12. Observed by Dr. Will Willimon, dean of the chapel at Duke University, in an article by the assistant editor of *Leadership,* Ed Rowel, entitled "Where Preaching Is Headed: Four Forces Shaping Tomorrow's Sermon," *Leadership* (winter 1997): 98.

13. From an interview with Leslie Newbigin by Tim Stafford entitled "God's Missionary to Us," *Christianity Today,* 9 December 1996, 29.

14. From an editorial by Timothy George, dean of Beeson Divinity School, entitled "Promoting Renewal, Not Tribalism," *Christianity Today,* 17 June 1996, 14.

15. George Ladd, *A Theology of the New Testament* (Grand Rapids: Eerdmans, 1974), 69.

16. Oswald Chambers, *My Utmost for His Highest* (Grand Rapids: Discovery House, 1995), reading for July 30.

Chapter 7: *H Stands for "Hop On!"*

1. This is a statement I have heard Dr. Lovelace make many times, but it is specifically quoted in an article entitled "Is a Global Great Awakening Just around the Corner?" *Christianity Today,* 14 November 1994, 80.

2. Robertson McQuilkin, "Six Inflammatory Questions: A Look at the Issues That Ignite Controversy," *Evangelical Missions Quarterly* (April 1994): 130–31.

3. This word picture was first suggested by Catherine Marshall in her book *Touching the Heart of God.*

4. A. W. Tozer in *Of God and Men,* quoted in the "Reflections" section of *Christianity Today,* 22 November 1993, 37.

Chapter 8: *O Stands for "Open Up!"*

1. William Pannell, professor of preaching and dean of the chapel at Fuller Theological Seminary, makes this observation in an article entitled "Polemic or Proclamation? The Art of Preaching in Today's World," *Fuller Focus* (fall 1996): 7.

2. From an interview with Tokumboh Adeyemo, Evangelical Missions Information Service, *World Pulse* (20 December 1996): 5.

3. See David Bryant, *Biblical Agendas: How to Use Scripture in Your Concert of Prayer* (Wheaton: Concerts of Prayer International, 1994), 16–49.

4. David Allen Hubbard, "Interpreting the Old Testament," *Theology News and Notes,* Fuller Theological Seminary (October 1995): 5.

Chapter 9: *P Stands for "Pray Back!"*

1. Quoted by E. M. Bounds in *Power through Prayer* (reprint, Atlanta: Operation Mobilization, 1989), 20.

2. See two publications by Concerts of Prayer International: *Operation Prayer: Two Exciting Formats for a Concert of Prayer,* 1986, 1994; and *Together in Hope: How to Conduct a Concert of Prayer Rally in Your City or Church,* 1995, which also includes video training tapes. Both are available from the COPI offices, P.O. Box 1399, Wheaton, IL 60189.

3. See David Bryant, *Creative Approaches to Concerts of Prayer: Techniques to Enliven and Enrich Your Concert of Prayer* (Wheaton: Concerts of Prayer International, 1994).

Chapter 10: *E Stands for "Enter In!"*

1. J. B. Phillips, *For This Day,* quoted in the "Reflections" section of *Christianity Today,* 14 November 1994, 56.

2. John Piper, *Future Grace* (Portland, Ore.: Multnomah, 1995). These words appear on the front cover and are expanded through thirty chapters that deal with practical issues from anxiety, to covetousness, to suffering and dying.

3. See the sixty-page small group discussion guide for David Bryant, *The Hope at Hand* published by Concerts of Prayer International (1995) and entitled *Take It to Your Friends.* Available through the COPI offices.

4. See the small group study guide in the concluding fifteen pages of David Bryant, *Stand in the Gap: How to Get Ready for the Coming World Revival,* rev. ed. (Ventura, Calif.: Regal, 1997).

For nearly twenty years, David Bryant has preached on revival and led mass prayer rallies in cities around the world. Founder and president of Concerts of Prayer International, he also serves as chairman for America's National Prayer Committee. He is the author of several books including *The Hope at Hand: National and World Revival for the Twenty-First Century.*